British Buses, Trams and Trolleybuses
1950s-1970s

British Buses, Trams and Trolleybuses 1950s-1970s

The operators and their vehicles
Part 6: London area and the South East Coast
Henry Conn

SLP

Silver Link Publishing Ltd

First published in 2011

British Library Cataloguing in Publication Data

A catalogue record for this book is available from the British Library.

ISBN 978 1 85794 387 0

Silver Link Publishing Ltd
The Trundle
Ringstead Road
Great Addington
Kettering
Northants NN14 4BW

Tel/Fax: 01536 330588
email: sales@nostalgiacollection.com
Website: www.nostalgiacollection.com

Printed and bound in the Czech Republic

All photographs not otherwise credited were taken by the author.

Title page: **The driver of London Transport trolleybus No 1525 shades his eyes from the very bright winter sunshine of 22 December 1960. The location is Archway, and No 1525 (FXH 525) is working on route 617 from North Finchley to Holborn. It is an L3 Class Metro-Cammell-bodied AEC, which was new in June 1940 and lasted to the end of the trolleybuses in May 1962.** *David Clarke*

Acknowledgements

Many of the photographs within this book have come from my collection, but my most sincere thanks go to David Clarke for allowing continuing and much-appreciated access to his wonderful collection of negatives and slides. David's portraits from the early 1950s through to the early 1960s of the buses, trams and trolleybuses of London Transport are rare and exceptional, and there are some wonderful views of trolleybuses in Hastings. Many thanks also to Geoff Gould, without whose time and commitment this book would not have been possible, and to Transport Treasury for safely archiving many of my negatives and slides.

The PSV Circle publications of all the operators illustrated, and many early issues of *Buses Illustrated*, were vital sources of information for this book.

Contents

Introduction

This volume concentrates primarily on London Transport, together with a number of larger operators and smaller independents who operated in or into London, and others from along the South Coast. Once again, I am indebted to David Clarke for his permission to include many of his wonderful portraits of London trams and trolleybuses. The trolleybus system is given extensive coverage in this volume, with views from almost all parts of the system dating from the summer of 1955 until the end in 1962.

David has also provided rare mid-1950s views of AEC Regals, Regents, a Guy, RLH 1, STLs, LTs and RM 1, which is seen in Marylebone Circus in February 1956. The Routemaster production spanned the years 1958 to 1968 and 2,760 were built. There was also one 'odd' Routemaster in service, FRM 1, the only rear-engined example, which had a transverse AEC AV691 rear engine and an entrance in the front overhang. This bus used some 60% of standard Routemaster parts and is illustrated in this volume working out of Potters Bar depot. The RT Class of AEC Regents was built for London Transport between 1939 and 1954, and bodywork for the post-war RT Class was built by five manufacturers, Cravens, Metro-Cammell, Park Royal, Saunders and Weymann. A total of 4,825 were produced in this period, and by the mid-1970s more than 600 were still in the operational fleet. The last RTs were to be found in Barking in 1979, the scene of the last regular RT operation by London Transport.

During the mid-1960s London Transport trialed the Leyland Atlantean and the Daimler Fleetline, ordering 117 of the latter, which entered service in 1970. A total of 2,646 Fleetlines were purchased, but with a quickly earned reputation of unreliability before the last was delivered,

London Transport confirmed that the whole class would be sold.

The AEC Regal RFs were solid buses and weighed 7½ tons, which was more than the RT. In the period 1951 to 1953 700 RFs were delivered, all bodied by Metro-Cammell, and their operation did not cease until 1979. A new fleet of single-deck buses arrived between 1967 and 1972; these were 665 11-metre-long AEC Merlins and 838 10-metre-long AEC Swifts. The Merlins had AEC 11.3-litre AH691 engines and the Swifts 8.2-litre AEC AH 505 engines. By 1975 most of the Merlins had been withdrawn and more than 350 were stored at an airfield at Radlett as buyers were sought.

London Transport purchased six Leyland Nationals and six Metro-Scanias and operated them on route S2 in Clapton. The Metro-Scanias were still being used in 1975, but had been withdrawn by 1976 and most were sold to Newport Corporation. Orders were placed for a total of 101 Leyland Nationals, which were two-door 36-seaters. In all, 506 Leyland Nationals were purchased by London Transport. The choice of bus on routes where physical restrictions or smaller passenger numbers dictated the use of smaller vehicles was the Bristol LH. They were just 9 metres long, and 95 were ordered in 1976 with ECW bodywork.

London Transport's green Country services, just before their take-over by London country bus services, had a fleet in excess of 1,200 buses and coaches, of which more than 900 were 15-plus years old. There were 484 RTs and 413 RF Regals, and the only rear-engined double-deck buses were eight Daimler Fleetlines and three Leyland Atlanteans.

There were a few small operators in the area served by London Transport. In Richmond, service 235 was provided by

Continental Pioneer, while Orpington & District ran from Croydon to Forestdale with a variety of second-hand buses. In Staines and Feltham, Golden Miller ran local services, again using a variety of second-hand vehicles, including an ex-Manchester Leyland Panther. Rover Bus Service ran between Chesham and Hemel Hempstead using Bedfords and Ford R series buses. Other independent operators featured in this volume are Elmtree Transport, Elms Coaches and North Downs Rural Transport.

Southdown Motor Services' routes stretched along the South Coast with depots in Portsmouth in the west to Eastbourne in the east. Services were coordinated with Portsmouth City Transport in the west and with Brighton Hove & District and Brighton Borough Transport. Brighton Hove & District came under Southdown control in 1969, and the combined fleet was over 800 strong. Southdown's fleet was well known for the distinctive Leyland PD3s with full-fronted Northern Counties bodies, and with the take-over of BH&D came significant numbers of ECW-bodied Bristols.

Brighton Borough Transport abandoned its red livery and by the mid-1970s all the buses were in the blue and white livery. More than half of the Brighton fleet were front-entrance Leyland Titans; the only single-deckers were Leyland Panther Cubs, which did not last long.

In Eastbourne the half-cab fleet consisted of AEC Regents and Leyland Titans. Between 1967 and 1971 Eastbourne purchased Daimler Roadliners and Leyland Panthers; the latter had a respectably long life at Eastbourne, compared to other operators of the bus.

Finally, Southern Motorways of Emsworth operated services around Emsworth and Petersfield, and operating the Emsworth service we include an excellent portrait of an ex-London Transport GS Class Guy Vixen.

Enjoy the nostalgia!

Bunching of buses is nothing new, and this view, taken in May 1973, shows three RTs working route 65, which at that time ran from Ealing through Kew, Richmond, Petersham, Ham, Kingston, Surbiton and Hook to Chessington Zoo. In Petersham, near the bottom of Star & Garter Hill, on the edge of Richmond Park, is RT 294 (HLX 111), an AEC Regent III fitted with a Park Royal roofbox body and new in January 1948. Initially allocated to Middle Row, it had a long service record, being allocated to Norwood, Shepherds Bush, Walworth, Hornchurch, Kingston, Wood Green, Enfield, Thornton Heath and Streatham. By 1972 it was allocated to Norbiton, which supplied the buses for route 65. RT 294 became a driver trainer in December 1973, was withdrawn in January 1977 and sold for scrap by July 1977. The last roofbox-bodied RT in service was RT 1903 in 1971, and the last used as a trainer was RT 4325, in November 1973. The nearest car sandwiched between two RTs is a Mark I Ford Escort.

Brighton Borough Transport

In 1938 an agreement between Brighton Corporation Transport Department and Brighton Hove & District Omnibus Company Ltd was reached whereby vehicles from both fleets would share a common livery of red with cream window surrounds and roof. A common fleet name, Brighton, Hove & District Transport, was adopted, and the Corporation vehicles carried the town crest. The agreement commenced on 1 April 1939, operating motorbuses and trolleybuses, pooling all receipts and sharing route mileage, 72.5% to BH&D, 27.5% to BCT. As part of the agreement, Brighton Corporation trams were phased out in August 1939. The agreement remained in place for 21 years.

On 18 November 1960 a new agreement was reached between Brighton Corporation, BH&D and Southdown, and the share of route mileage and revenue was 20.5%, 50.5% and 29% respectively. The operating area was known as the Brighton Area Transport Services (BATS) and encompassed both Brighton and Hove together with adjoining communities such as Shoreham and Rottingdean. The BATS Agreement, as it became known, was operational from 1 January 1961 and would last for the next 24 years.

In 1961 Brighton Corporation operated a fleet of trolleybuses and motorbuses from its Lewes Road bus depot. As part of the Agreement the trolleybus system

The year is 1964, the month is August, and the bus nearest the camera is No 84 (HUF 84), a Weymann-bodied AEC Regent III. A batch of eight were delivered to Brighton Corporation in 1947, Nos 81 to 88 (HUF 81 to HUF 88), and they were fitted with AEC A208 9.6-litre engines. No 84 was withdrawn and scrapped by Cooper of Ringmer in 1967. Passing is a Northern Counties-bodied Leyland PD3/4, while on the right can be seen a Ford Anglia, the nose of a Triumph Herald and the boots of a Mini and a Vauxhall Victor FC. The hotel in the background is the Royal Albion. Designed by Amon Henry Wilds, it opened for business on 27 July 1826. It was originally a four-storey building with impressive Corinthian and Ionic columns with a large Doric porch. The hotel faces inward, away from the sea, as guests preferred to look at the gardens of the Royal Pavilion, which extended onto Old Steine. In 1847 the hotel was renamed the Royal Albion, and the original now forms the eastern side of the building, while the present hotel comprises a number of different edifices that have been completed over the years into a single structure of meandering corridors and staircases.

was to be abandoned, and the last trolley ran on 30 June 1961. The motorbus fleet at this time consisted of rear-entrance, open-platform double-deckers, comprising 10 AEC Regent Is, 14 AEC Regent IIIs, all with Weymann bodywork, and 20 Leyland Titan PD2s with Metro-Cammell Weymann Orion bodywork. On order were further Leyland PD2s, but with forward-entrance bodies.

Just about to depart on service 26A to Preston Grove in 1962 is No 91 (KCD 91), one of a batch of six Weymann-bodied AEC Regent IIIs – Nos 89 to 94 (KCD 89 to KCD 94) – delivered in 1949. This bus was the last AEC to leave the Lewes Road depot, on tow to the scrapyard on 10 May 1969. The Bristol behind intrigues me, as I am unable to positively identify it. I think it is one of the open-top convertibles belonging to Brighton, Hove & District, probably from the batch XPM 41 to 44.

Between March and April 1959 Brighton Corporation took delivery of 20 Weymann-bodied Leyland PD2/37s. They were Nos 51 to 59 and 70 to 80 (WCD 51 to WCD 59 and WCD 70 to WCD 80). This is No 51 (WCD 51) working service 52 to Goldstone Crescent at Old Steine, with St James Street in the background, in the autumn of 1967. The back end of a car, just visible to the right of the bus, is I think a Citroen Safari; first produced in 1959, it remained in production until 1975. Behind the Citroen is a Sunbeam Talbot 90, probably a Mark III, which was marketed as the Sunbeam Supreme.

Above: **Descending Widdicombe Way in Bevendean in May 1972, still wearing the red and cream livery of the combined fleets of Brighton Corporation and Brighton, Hove & District, is No 51 (WCD 51). This bus was re-numbered 75 in November 1973 and became a driver trainer vehicle, remaining in this role until January 1981. I believe it is now under long-term restoration.**

Below: **Working service 49A to Southwick in the autumn of 1967, crossing the St James Street junction, is No 80 (WCD 80), numerically the last of the Weymann-bodied Leyland PD2/37s that arrived in the early spring of 1959. To the right is a Bedford CA panel van, which with its distinctive 'pug nose' was in production from 1952 until 1969. The lorry in the left distance is also a Bedford, a TK.**

Above: No 5 (5005 CD) is working service 7 to Ovingdean in July 1966. It is a Weymann-bodied Leyland PD2/37 that was new to Brighton Corporation in June 1961. It was withdrawn in May 1977 and sold to Messrs Lowe of Baronsworth Farm, Mereworth, then in April 1985 it was acquired by Tentrek of Sidcup, and was later noted at a Carlton dealer in August 1988. London Bus Export acquired the bus and converted it to an open-top, exporting it to Preben Paaske in Copenhagen for use as a vintage sightseeing bus. The parked cars in the background include, nearest the camera, a Morris/Austin 1800, a Vauxhall Victor FB and on the left, with the boot lid open, a Ford Cortina Mark I.

Left: This is another of the Weymann-bodied Leyland PD2/37s new in the summer of 1961. No 12 (5012 CD) is working service 49A to East Moulsecoomb. This bus was withdrawn and sold by April 1978 to Cross Roads Travel, which sold it a few months later to Shadwell of Warrington. In December 1979 the bus was noted with Tameside Venture Scouts, then with Runcorn Scouts by July 1980. By the early 1990s it was a training bus with COST in Runcorn, but had been scrapped by 1995.

Above: **This is Old Steine in Brighton in May 1972, and No 16 (5016 CD) was the last, numerically, of the 16 Weymann-bodied Leyland PD2/37s that arrived during June and July 1961. No 16 was withdrawn in April 1978 and saw further service with Cross Roads Travel of Warrington until December 1979.**

In the background, to the right, is one of the Leyland Panthers new to Brighton in late 1968 and early 1969. Behind No 16 is one of the ten Northern Counties Daimler CRG6LXs that were ordered by Brighton, Hove & District and delivered between December 1969 and March 1970.

Left: **Working the Brighton Station circular route 42 in May 1972 is No 25 (25 CCD), which was one of three front-entrance Leyland PD2/37s, Nos 25 to 27 (25 to 27 CCD), with Weymann bodywork, new in July 1963. This bus was withdrawn in July 1978 and passed into further service with Thomas Brothers of Clydach Vale until 1981. In March 1970 Brighton Corporation Transport adopted a new livery of blue and white, chosen to reflect the sea and white cliffs and in response to a number of complaints from the public that did not relate to the Corporation, but rather to BH&D, so as to differentiate between the two operators.**

Right: **Working route 39 to Saltdean Mount in the summer of 1966 is No 26 (26 CCD), another of the Weymann-bodied Leyland PD2/37 new to Brighton Corporation in July 1963. No 26 was withdrawn in 1978 and sold to Cross Roads Travel in April 1978, lasting only until October of that year before being sold to HRQ Coaches of Tyldesley; by March of the following year it had been sold to Askin's of Barnsley, which scrapped it from July 1979. The car in the background is a Fiat 500, and the Rail Freight lorry is, I think, a Commer.**

Below: **October 1965 saw the arrival of the last batch of Weymann-bodied Leyland PD2/37s. They were Nos 17 to 20 (DCD 17C to 20C), and seen in Western Road in May 1972 is the last-numbered. This bus was withdrawn in March 1982 and noted with Parks of Hamilton in May 1983, but had been sold for scrap by November 1983. Hanningtons was the most prestigious shopping address in Brighton,** but by the 1980s the store was well past its prime, gradually losing ground to the stores in Western Road and Churchill Square and competition from out-of-town stores with lower prices and free parking. The owners, the Hunnisett family, sold the store to Regina Estates in September 2000 for £20 million. The following June, after 193 years trading, the store closed its doors for the last time.

Above: **The last half-cab double-deckers delivered to Brighton Corporation arrived during the months of June and July 1968. They were Nos 31 to 35 (LUF 131F to 133F and MCD 134F to 135F) and had bodywork by Metro-Cammell Weymann. Seen in Western Road on 20 March 1976 is No 134 (MCD 134F). This bus was converted to an open-top in 1979 and sold by the Corporation in 1993. It was noted working with London Pride in April 1995.**

Below: **Working the Goldstone Valley to Old Steine service in May 1972 is No 137 (NUF 137G). Between December 1968 and January 1969 Brighton took delivery of seven Leyland Panther Cub PSRC1/1s with dual doors. The first three, Nos 136 to 138, (NUF 136G to 138G), were bodied by Strachan.**

Above: The remainder of the Panther Cubs, Nos 139 to 142 (NUF 139G to 142G), were bodied by Marshall. I quite liked the Strachan-bodied examples, but all were almost universally disliked by Brighton Corporation and their working lives were short, all being withdrawn and sold by October 1975 to North in Leeds. No 142 (NUF 142G), seen in Old Steine in May 1972, had the distinction of being the last Panther Cub built for the UK market.

Below: The first rear-engine buses delivered to Brighton Corporation were five Leyland PDR1A/1s with Willowbrook dual-doorway bodywork. They were numbered 81 to 85 (TUF 81J to 85J) and arrived in 1971. Seen when only a few months old in Old Steine is No 81 (TUF 81J). After receiving an East Lancashire front after a minor accident, it was sold to G&G Coaches in February 1983, then passed to Red Watch in East Calder in August 1987. It was noted at the yard of Dunsmore of Larkhall in July 1990, and was subsequently purchased by David Mulpeter in August 2001. Unfortunately, due to severe chassis corrosion, the bus was scrapped in 2004.

Brighton, Hove & District

The Brighton, Hove & Preston United Omnibus Company was formed on 12 September 1884 to amalgamate the interests of the major horse bus operators in Brighton, and in 1901 the company decided the time was right to begin replacing the horse buses with motor buses. By 1910 there were around 40 buses in operation. In February 1915 the buses of Thomas Tilling commenced working on a service between Portslade Station and Castle Square, Brighton, and on 22 November 1916 Thomas Tilling Ltd purchased the urban routes of the Brighton, Hove & Preston United company.

By 1922 Tilling was operating between Portslade and Kemp Town, Sackville Road and Castle Square, Hove Station and Kemp Town, Old Steine and Rottingdean, Old Steine and Patcham, Portslade and Brighton Station, and Hove Station and Kemp Town. Although several attempts were made at coordinating services within the Brighton area, nothing came to fruition and eventually, on 26 November 1935, the Brighton, Hove & District Omnibus Company was incorporated as a wholly owned subsidiary of Thomas Tilling Ltd.

In July 1937 Brighton Council and the company finally reached an agreement on coordination, which provided for the pooling of receipts and running expenses in the ratio of 72½% to the company and 27½% to the Corporation. The agreement was confirmed by Act of Parliament in 1938. A joint operating area came into force on 1 April 1939 covering Brighton, Hove, Portslade, Rottingdean and Southwick, although Southdown Motor Services routes within the borough were not included.

The introduction of joint working heralded the end of the Corporation tramway system and the first closure took place in April 1939 when motor buses commenced running between Old Steine and Tivoli Crescent North, replacing the trams on the Dyke Road route. On 1 May 1939 trolleybuses of Brighton Corporation replaced more tram routes, although it was not until 1945 that Brighton, Hove & District trolleybuses were seen in the borough when the Black Rock to Race Hill section was wired for use. The trolleybuses had actually been delivered in 1939, but had been stored for the duration of the war at Whitehawk depot and their introduction made BH&D unique as the only Tilling group company that operated trolleybuses.

When the war ended a number of new routes were opened to keep pace with the construction of new housing estates on the outskirts of Brighton. The large Hollingbury Estate was wired for trolleybuses during 1951 and finally opened in September of that year, although BH&D did not operate on the route. On 24 March 1959 the trolleybus routes in the eastern part of Brighton ceased operations and the BH&D trolleybuses were withdrawn. A few months later in May 1959 BH&D became the last Tilling group company to place the Bristol Lodekka into service, when Nos 4 and 5 commenced operating on the route between Pool Valley and Coombe Road. Of the eight Lodekkas delivered, Nos 1 to 3 had convertible open-top bodywork, while the remainder had normal bodywork.

Towards the end of 1960 negotiations with Southdown Motor Services were completed, and from 1 January 1961 a new joint agreement between Brighton Corporation, Brighton, Hove & District and Southdown came into force. In 1962 the Brighton, Hove & District Company became a part of the Transport Holding Company, which had been formed in an attempt to reorganise the nationalised bus companies. BH&D had been a nationalised bus company since the Tilling group had sold its interests to the British Transport Commission in 1948 and, when the BET Group was acquired in 1968, Southdown Motor Services joined the nationalised companies. With the formation of the National Bus Company on 1 January 1969, Brighton, Hove & District was merged with its larger brother, combining operations in the Brighton area, and the company became dormant for the time being.

During 1952 Brighton, Hove & District received 13 ECW-bodied Bristol KSWs. Nos 6430 to 6436 (GNJ 995 to 998 and GNJ 991 to 993) were delivered with Bristol engines, and the remainder, Nos 6437 to 6442 (GPM 500 to 502 and GPM 900 to 902) had Gardner engines. All these buses were renumbered in 1955, losing the '6', and representing the Gardner-engined batch is No 442 (GPM 902), which is seen in Conway Street in Hove in 1968, shortly before its withdrawal from service.

Above: During 1954 two batches of ECW-bodied Bristol KSW6Gs were purchased by Brighton, Hove & District. The second batch were numbered 6462 to 6467 (JAP 500 to JAP 505), and seen working service 43 to the West Pier in the late autumn of 1967 is the now renumbered 463 (JAP 501). Due to the fact that BH&D operated almost exclusively within built-up urban areas, the company retained more of a municipal flavour than most Tilling fleets. In the background of this lovely view is the Royal Albion Hotel, and the entrance to Pool Valley is behind the bus on the other side of the road.

Below: Nos 6468 to 6476 (JAP 506 to JAP 514), ECW-bodied Bristol KSW6Gs, followed in 1955. This view of No 475 (JAP 513) was taken in the early summer of 1967 while taking a rest from service 26. In the background to the right is a lovely contrast of a relatively new Ford Corsair and a relatively elderly Vauxhall Cresta E. The latter was launched in 1954 and had a 2,262cc six-cylinder engine and a choice of leather or fabric upholstery, optional two-tone paintwork, a heater as standard, a small electric fascia-mounted clock, a cigar-lighter, a lamp automatically illuminating the boot when opened, and a vanity mirror on the inside of the front passenger's sun-visor, together with a special ornamental badge above the V (for Vauxhall) badge on the nose of the car. A Cresta tested by the British magazine *The Motor* in 1956 had a top speed of 82.2mph and could accelerate from 0 to 60mph in 20.2 seconds.

Above: The operating area was within urban areas that had no low bridges, which meant that the company would gain notoriety in being the last customer for the Bristol KS double-decker in 1957. This last batch were ECW-bodied, 7ft 6in wide Bristol KS6Gs, numbered 493 to 500 (MPM 493 to MPM 500). Working service 55 to Upper Portslade in the autumn of 1967 is No 495 (MPM 495).

Below: When the first Bristol Lodekkas entered service in 1959 the numbering series started from 1. The eight new ECW-bodied Bristol LDS6Gs looked very different from the Bristol KSs, particularly with the dispensing of the exposed radiator for a new fibreglass front. The engine was also new, a Bristol 8.4-litre six-cylinder BVW engine. These buses also featured a pair of radiators either side of the front destination screen for the Cave-Browne-Cave combined heating and ventilation system. The rear axle had air suspension and the first three, Nos 1 to 3 (OPN 801 to OPN 803), were fitted with convertible open-top bodywork and were painted an all-over cream livery. The remaining five, Nos 4 to 8 (OPN 804 to 808) received the fleet livery of red and cream. The summer of 1959 was hot, and this, coupled with slow running speeds, overwhelmed the ventilation system, which resulted in warm air being blown into both saloons. This was sorted by fitting conventional fans, as well as the updated Lodekka grills. Nos 4 to 7 were withdrawn in 1972, and No 8 was withdrawn in 1974. The convertibles lasted two more years, then passed to Hants & Dorset for further service. This is Old Steine in the summer of 1967, and nearest the camera is No 4 (OPN 804); standing next to it is Brighton Corporation No 54 (WCD 54), a Weymann-bodied Leyland PD2/37, which was new in early 1959.

Above: **Between April and June 1960 17 Bristol FS6Bs were added to the BH&D fleet as Nos 9 to 25 (RPN 9 to 20 and SPM 21 to 25).** Proving satisfactory, the six-cylinder Bristol BVW engine was fitted to these buses and, learning from the initial teething troubles associated with the LDS type, conventional radiators and grilles were fitted. The Cave-Browne-Cave heating/ventilation system was not adopted but additional under-seat fan heaters were introduced on these vehicles. In common with other BTC fleets, the Tilling 'T'-style destination boxes were fitted. As with the previous batch of Lodekkas, there was a mixture of both closed-top and convertible open-top bodywork. Initial allocations were Nos 12 and 13 joining the closed-top LDSs on the busy 38 between West Street and Coombe Road, while Nos 14 to 20 worked cross-town route No 1 between Portslade and Lintott Avenue, displacing Bristol K5Gs, and were the first 8-foot-wide vehicles to see regular use in the narrow Kemp Town area. Nos 24 and 25 were allocated to routes 15 between Upper Portslade and Patcham and 15B Mile Oak to Patcham respectively. The convertibles, Nos 9 to 11, 21 and 22, were painted in the cream livery with black bonnets and mudguards and joined the LDS open-top trio, Nos 1 to 3 on the seafront service 17, replacing 1940-vintage Bristol K5Gs. Following a number of complaints from elderly passengers, No 23 underwent modification to the platform in January 1961, whereby a half-step was incorporated offering a lower platform floor nearest the rear axle. Favourable reports from passengers resulted in all other 1960 FSs and the eight LDS buses being similarly modified. Saloon lighting was also improved by the use of fluorescent tubes, introduced on the later FSFs, so these vehicles were converted from tungsten bulbs early in their careers.

Below: **Between 1961 and 1962 Brighton, Hove & District purchased 15 ECW-bodied Bristol FSFs ('Flat Floor Short Forward Entrance'), the 27-foot version of the FLF.** The largest operator of this relatively rare marque of bus was Central SMT, which purchased 48. The last batch of Bristol FSFs to arrive were Nos 36 to 40 (WNJ 36 to 40), and they were delivered with Bristol engines. The driver of No 40 (WNJ 40) is assisting the conductress by using the external handles to change the front destination blinds at Old Steine in May 1972. The FSFs were the first vehicles in the fleet to feature driver-operated platform doors and fluorescent lighting. Another innovation fitted to Nos 31-40 was offside illuminated advertisement panels. Due to the restricted lower saloon layout, which was not popular with passengers and crews alike, the FSFs never settled to a regular route, and at least one was allocated to each main route. All the FSFs were withdrawn and sold by 1975.

Above: **Also arriving in 1962 were ten Bristol FSs, Nos 41 to 50, the first five of which had Gardner engines and the remainder Bristol engines. Nos 41 to 44 (XPM 41 to 44) arrived between March and April 1962, and were convertible open-toppers. Working the Sea Front Service on Marine Parade in May 1972 is No 42 (XPM 42). The bus is surrounded by an interesting selection of vehicles, which include the back of a Ford Capri, a Vauxhall Viva HB, a Vauxhall Viva HA van and a Gosport & Fareham Guy Arab.**

Below: **The red and cream livery was introduced on 1 April 1939. The first Lodekkas**

for BH&D entered service in 1959, the same year as the trolleybuses were withdrawn. Seen in Brighton heading for the downs of Race Hill on a hot summer's day in 1970 is BH&D No 55 (4655 AP), one of three ECW-bodied Bristol FS6Gs new in September 1963. Behind the bus is a Volvo 140 series, which was built in Torslanda between 1967 and 1974. Also visible is a Morris Minor 1000 and a Vauxhall Viva HA van, which was known as the Bedford 8 or 10cwt van. The van remained in production until 1983 and thousands were purchased by the Post Office and British Telecom.

Right: **Standing outside the depot in Conway Street, Hove, in the early spring of 1972 is No 52 (AAP 52B), one of four ECW-bodied Bristol FS6Bs with convertible open tops that arrived between January and April 1964. Nos 53 and 54 differed from the rest of the convertible fleet in that, originally, they were painted red and cream, as opposed to all-over cream, this pair being used on a new circular tour service.**

Below: **Between January and August 1965 11 ECW-bodied Bristol FSs, Nos 62 to 72, were delivered. Nos 62 to 64 and 68 to 70 were fitted with Bristol engines, and the remainder had Gardner engines. Working service 1A to Portslade Station in the early spring of 1967 is No 65 (DPM 65C). The disappearing car on the left is a Vauxhall Viva HB. I liked the HB's handsome lines and its peppy performance, and the body design had improved following Vauxhall's poor reputation with corrosion on previous models. The HB had better** underbody protection, but UK cars were still prone to rusting through the front wings in the area behind the headlights, where water, mud and salt could accumulate. My father's Vauxhall HB estate was the first car I learned to drive, and I drove it all the way from Rotterdam to Denmark and back again.

Above: **During 1969 several ex-Brighton, Hove & District buses received Southdown livery. Traversing Old Steine in this livery in May 1972 is No 69 (ENJ 69C), one of three ECW-bodied Bristol FS6Bs, Nos 68 to 70, that arrived in April 1965. Behind No 69 is one of the Corporation's Willowbrook-bodied Leyland PDR1A/1s, while partially visible in the background is an Aston Martin. Buses Nos 58 to 61 and the 1965 intake, Nos 62 to 72, introduced manually operated platform doors, but at the expense of the half-step platform welcomed by less able passengers. The distinctive triple route number blind specified by BH&D on earlier deliveries was also absent from these final 15 vehicles, which were to be the last rear-entrance buses.**

Below: **In all, Brighton, Hove & District purchased 20 ECW-bodied Bristol FLFs, all with Gardner engines. Representing a batch of six delivered between January and August 1966 is No 78 (HPN 78D), seen here in Old Steine in May 1972. All of the FLFs were fitted with the Cave-Browne-Cave heating system, and Tilling 'T'-type front destination screens. 'T'-type destinations were also fitted to the rear of Nos 74 and 75, Nos 73 and 76 to 92 having inverted rear screens where the number blind was positioned above the ultimate destination blind. During BH&D ownership the FLFs were mainly allocated to routes 2, 5 and the 26/46 group, although certain peak-hour journeys on routes 1, 6 and 54 were also worked by these vehicles. It was FLF No 75 that would operate the very last BH&D journey on 31 December 1968. The car is a Ford Cortina Mark I.**

Right: **The last Bristol half-cab double-deck buses delivered new to Brighton, Hove & District arrived between January and March 1967 in the form of a batch of 10 ECW-bodied Bristol FLF6Gs, Nos 83 to 92 (KPM 83E to 92E). Seen approaching Old Steine in Brighton in the summer of 1967 is No 87 (KPM 87E). The newest FLFs, Nos 85 to 92, left their home town in 1973 as part of the National Bus Company/Scottish Bus Group FLF/VR exchange, still in the red and cream**

livery. The remainder continued to operate on former BH&D routes until withdrawal and sale during 1977 and 1978. On the right is a Mark I Mini, which first appeared in April 1959; between then and 1967 more than 1,190,000 were produced. Is the scooter a Vespa or Lambretta? Brighton, to my mind, has always been synonymous with the scooter.

Below: **This is numerically the last Bristol FLF6G new to Brighton, Hove & District, No 92 (KPM 92E), seen working service 26 to Mile**

Oak in the summer of 1967. At the merger with Southdown on 1 January 1969 the BH&D fleet comprised 160 buses: Lodekkas Nos 1 to 92, REs Nos 201 to 210, KSWs Nos 426, 442 to 445, 447 to 483 and 485 to 492, and KSs Nos 493 to 500. The KSW vehicles Nos 426, 443 to 445, 447 to 449, 451, 462 and 466 were not operated, passing to Southdown as withdrawn vehicles, while No 442 was in use as a driver training vehicle. Southdown renumbered the entire BH&D fleet, adding 2000 to the existing fleet numbers.

Right: **Between December 1969 and March 1970 ten Northern Counties-bodied Daimler CRG6LXs were delivered, Nos 2103 to 2112 (PUF 203H to 212H), and entered service with the BH&D division in April 1970 in red and cream livery. Unlike 'true' BH&D vehicles, the wheels were painted red (initially polished guard-ring discs also being fitted to the front wheels), and the vehicles featured fleet names on the vehicle fronts below the windscreen. Upon delivery, these buses were the largest double-deckers in Brighton, and initially all ten were allocated to routes 11 (Portslade, Mill House-Hangleton) and 54 (Old Steine-Hangleton Sunninghill Estate), allowing partial conversion of these two routes to one-man operation, although two workings remained crew-operated. Seen here working the 54 in May 1972 is No 2103 (PUF 203H).**

Below: **The last ten vehicles to enter service with BH&D were ten ECW-bodied Bristol RESLs in August and September 1968. Being the first single-deckers in the fleet since 1947, a new numbering series was started, the REs becoming 201 to 210 (PPM 201G to 210G). These vehicles introduced the semi-automatic gearbox to the fleet and were the first rear-engine vehicles purchased. Initially Nos 201 to 203 were allocated to route 8 (Hangleton Hardwick Rd-Brighton Rail Station) from 8 August 1968. Nos 204 to 210 were allocated to routes 43/44/44A (Black Rock/Race Hill-Old Steine), commencing on 8 September 1968. However, from 25 May 1969, under Southdown ownership, the REs** were reallocated to routes 11 (Hangleton-Portslade) and 54 (Old Steine-Hangleton). On 12 April, the REs were again reallocated to route 37/37A (Kemp Town-Hove/Southwick). Southdown allocated three further RESLs, ordered by BH&D, and these were slightly longer and had curved windscreens. They were Nos 2211 to 2213, and the first two were immediately allocated to route 37. Number 2213 was initially delivered in Southdown livery and numbered 600, but remained de-licensed for five months before a repaint into the red and cream livery. This bus had the distinction of being the only vehicle to be repainted from green to red. Seen at Hove railway station in May 1972 is No 2211 (TCD 611J).

Continental Pioneer

Industrial action by London Transport crews in 1966 led to the temporary suspension of some minor routes, a few of which were not reinstated by London Transport, allowing private operators to take them over. The short 235 service between Richmond Station and Richmond Hill, requiring just one bus, was such an example, and Isleworth Coaches operated it from 1966 until May 1968, when it was taken over by Continental Pioneer, a firm more used to catering for the European holiday market. In 1980 London Transport rerouted its then 71 service via Richmond Hill, removing the need for the 235, and the coincidental loss of Continental Pioneer's cheap rented base in Richmond, when the land was redeveloped, saw the demise of that company.

Former London Transport RF-type single-deckers were used and MLL 795, once RF 258, is seen in Richmond on a Saturday afternoon in November 1969 working the 235. This particular bus was originally a 2RF2/1 Green Line coach and was new in June 1952. Through a busy 12-year service life it worked from Swanley, Garston, Epping, Hertford, St Albans and Luton depots. It was withdrawn in April 1964 and later that year was sold to PVS of Upminster. By the beginning of 1965 it had been purchased by Premier Travel of Cambridge, and was with that company until September 1969. Continental purchased MLL 795 in September 1969 and it worked the 235 route until withdrawal in June 1971.

Eastbourne Corporation

Eastbourne was the first Corporation in the world to receive consent for a motor bus service, and this commenced operating in April 1903. The first bus to operate the service was a 14-seat Milnes Daimler, and from then until the 1930s buses used included Clarkson steam buses, open-top De Dion Boutons and gearless Leyland Titans. Mostly Leylands were purchased in the 1930s, then just after the war Crossleys and Bruce-bodied AEC Regents were delivered. Eastbourne was a keen purchaser of Bruce Coach Works-bodied buses, the very last being purchased in 1951. The Bruce factory closed in December 1951, and thereafter Eastbourne stayed loyal to East Lancashire designs for many years. The conversion of many older buses in the fleet to open-toppers resulted in many quite old buses lasting well beyond their sell-by date. A number of liveries were used by Eastbourne, including blue and primrose, with the open-top buses being painted white. From 1968 the blue and primrose was replaced by cream with light blue lining, and by 1974 this had been replaced by a darker blue and deeper cream.

In August 1939 Eastbourne Corporation took delivery of five all-Leyland Lion LT8s, numbered 11 to 15 (JK 8417 to JK 8421). They were the last petrol-engined buses to be acquired by Eastbourne and all but one of the batch were requisitioned for military service. No 12 (JK 8418), seen here, remained and in 1954 received an 8.6-litre oil engine from an ex-Southdown 1935-vintage Leyland TS7 Tiger. In 1963 it was re-seated to a 43-seater in 1963 and was the last Leyland Lion in municipal service, being withdrawn in June 1967. This view was taken just before withdrawal, and the bus is now in preservation.

In July 1936 Eastbourne took delivery of three all-Leyland TD4Cs, Nos 94 to 96 (JK 5604 to JK 5606), which had torque converters and petrol engines. In the early 1950s the Corporation purchased 12 buses from Southdown in order to use their 8.6-litre Leyland diesel engines, and during 1953 all three buses received these. No 94 was rebuilt to an open-topper in 1952 and named 'White Heather', and No 96 was rebuilt to open-top in 1954 and named 'The White King'. This is the foot of Beachy Head in July 1961, and seen working the Sea Front service is No 96 (JK 5606). It was withdrawn from service in May 1963 and sold to Creamline of Bordon to be used as a tree-lopper; it was noted lying derelict by September of that year.

Above: **Between October 1946 and May 1947 Eastbourne received six East Lancashire-bodied Leyland PD1s, Nos 13 to 18 (JK 9111 to JK 9116). Apart from No 15 all were converted to open-top, and No 18 (JK 9116) is seen here working route 6 during the summer of 1967. No 16 was used as a training bus during the early part of 1962, but was back in service by September of that year. Between October 1962 and July 1963 it was rebuilt to an open-topper and remained in service until withdrawal in January 1968; it was noted as scrapped in October 1976.**

Below: **Delivered to Eastbourne in February 1948 were three Leyland PD2/1s, which were assembled by Air Dispatch (Coachbuilders) at Cardiff, renamed Bruce Coach Works in September 1948. The trio were numbered 25 to 27 (JK 9982 to JK 9984), and this is No 27 (JK 9984) turning onto Grove Road in the summer of 1967, just a short time before its withdrawal from service in February 1968.**

Above: **This depot view was taken in the early summer of 1966, and contains a good deal of interest. From the left, the first two buses are Nos 29 and 30 (JK 9986 and JK 9987), part of a batch of four AEC Regent IIIs delivered in April 1948; they were the first buses to be delivered with bodies made by Bruce Coach Works, and the first built to a four-bay design. No 23 (JK 9651), the third bus seen here, was part of a batch of five Weymann-bodied AEC Regent IIIs new to Eastbourne in May 1947. On the right is 'Polly' (HCD 447), an ECW-bodied Leyland PS1/1 new to Southdown as its No 1247 in 1947. It was sold to Eastbourne Corporation Welfare Department in 1961 and replaced a Dennis, No 81 (FUF 181). All three AEC Regent IIIs were withdrawn from service in April 1966, with No 29 passing to the Southdown Gliding Club, where the engine was used as a glider winch; the other two were scrapped.**

Below: **Delivered to Eastbourne in July 1950 was this AEC Regal, originally No 11 (AHC 411), with East Lancashire dual-purpose 30-seat rear-entrance bodywork. It had a 7.7-litre engine and a crash gearbox, and was intended for private hire, but was often used for relief bus duties. It was originally painted blue and primrose, but was repainted in the late 1960s in a livery of cream with a blue stripe. No 11 was renumbered 93 in 1970, and is seen here in the depot on 26 September 1975. The bus was withdrawn in April 1978, but was subsequently repurchased by the Corporation in 1992, and was restored to full PSV status.**

Above: **Seven East Lancashire-bodied AEC Regent Vs arrived between March and May 1956, numbered 49 to 55 (DHC 649 to 655). Working service 4 to Ocklynge in November 1966 is No 49 (DHC 649), which together with Nos 50 and 51 entered service on Good Friday 1956. No 49 was loaned to London Country between January and June 1976. It was also the last of this batch of Regent Vs to be withdrawn, in August 1980, and was noted at Sykes of Barnsley's yard in September of that year. The B-registered car is a Ford Anglia 105E, which was introduced in 1959. The car had a 997cc engine and acceleration was somewhat sluggish. It also had a four-speed manual gearbox with synchromesh on the top three ratios. This was replaced by a new gearbox with synchromesh on all gears in September 1962, with 1198cc-engined cars. The acceleration of a 998cc engine was noted as being 0 to 60 in 29.9 seconds.**

Below: **Between May and June 1961 the Corporation took delivery of five AEC Regent Vs with East Lancashire bodies, Nos 56 to 60 (HJK 156 to 160). They were 27 feet long, 8 feet wide, had 9.6-litre engines, and the chassis cost £2,768 each. They were delivered in cream and light blue livery and the upper deck had translucent roof panels and full-drop opening windows. Three of the batch, Nos 56, 59 and 60, had platform doors fitted during 1968 for use on Town Tours. Working that service along the 2½-mile-long Grand Parade in May 1972 is No 56 (HJK 156).**

Above: **Passing Eastbourne railway station in May 1972 is No 60 (HJK 160), another of the batch of AEC Regent Vs delivered during May and June 1961. Platform doors were fitted for Town Tour duties in September 1968. The bus was loaned to London Country during May 1976, and was allocated to Reigate. It was withdrawn in September 1978 and had been scrapped by December of that year. The interesting line-up of cars at the entrance to the station includes a Volkswagen 'Beetle', a Rover 2000 and a Jaguar.**

Below: **Another five East Lancashire-bodied AEC Regent Vs arrived in July 1962, Nos 61 to 65 (JJK 261 to 265). They were delivered in blue and primrose livery, with a paler blue than used in previous buses, but were repainted in the normal blue livery during 1965 and 1966. No 63 (JJK 263) is seen at Eastbourne railway station in May 1972 with the cream and light blue livery that was first applied during 1968-69. It was withdrawn in June 1979 and was noted with Rollinson of Carlton in November of that year.**

Above: Between March and April 1966 Eastbourne took delivery of ten East Lancashire-bodied Leyland PD2A/30s, all of which had entered service by May of that year. They were Nos 71 to 80, (BJK 671D to 680D) and had St Helens-style front grilles; they were delivered in blue and primrose livery and were the first buses to have separate number blinds. This view of No 72 (BJK 672D) passing Eastbourne station was taken in September 1967. Behind is No 17 (JK 9115), an East Lancashire-bodied Leyland PD1, which was converted to open-top between November 1962 and February 1963, and withdrawn in February 1968. No 72 was withdrawn in January 1983, and both are now in preservation.

Below: A further five East Lancashire-bodied Leyland PD2A/30s with St Helens-style tin-front grilles, Nos 81 to 85 (DHC 781E to 785E) followed in June 1967. These were the last new rear-entrance buses purchased by Eastbourne, and the last to be delivered with the blue and primrose livery. Representing this batch is No 83 (DHC 783E), which is seen at Cornfield Road roundabout in May 1972. The car in the background is a Ford Escort Mark I.

Above: With the banning of rear-entrance double-deckers for bus grants, Eastbourne joined in the search for alternatives, and tried the newly developed rear-engined single-deckers in the late 1960s; five Daimler Roadliner SRC6s arrived during 1967 and 1968. Leyland produced a Strachan-bodied dual-doorway demonstrator for the 1966 Earls Court show, and this was YTB 771D, which in 1967 became Eastbourne's No 92, the sole Panther Cub in the fleet. No 88 (EJK 888F), seen here at Cornfield Road roundabout in the spring of 1972, was one of three East Lancashire dual-doorway Leyland Panther PSUR1/1R single-deckers delivered during June and July 1968. These buses were better than the Roadliners, and the detested Panther Cub, but were still extremely unpopular with the drivers.

Right: Another ten East Lancashire-bodied dual-doorway Leyland PSUR1A/1s arrived between October 1970 and February 1971, numbered 1 to 10 (HHC 901J to 910J). Seen on 26 September 1975 at Eastbourne railway station is No 2 (HHC 902J). The Panther chassis was designed for single-deck passenger

vehicles 10.97 metres long and 2.44 metres wide, and the engine and gearbox units were situated behind the rear axle. The bus chassis had a dropped frame forward of the rear axle to allow for the fitting of low, single-step-entry-and-exit bodies. The springs were suitable for a gross laden weight of 12,192kg distributed as 4,064kg on the front axle and 8,128kg on the rear.

Elms Coaches

Another service that passed to a private operator in the 1960s, this time in north-west London, was the 98B, which was transferred to Elms Coaches on 15 June 1968. The service, between Rayners Lane and Ruislip, followed a somewhat indirect route, linking several residential areas not otherwise served by bus.

ECW-bodied Bristol LS buses were preferred by Elms Coaches, and former United Automobile PHN 831 is seen in Headstone Lane operating the 98B in July 1969, apparently still in its previous owner's red livery. This bus entered service with United as its No BU2 in May 1953 and remained in service until late 1967. It was noted with W. Norths of Sherburn-in-Elmet in January 1968 **before being purchased by Elms Coaches and entering service in February 1968. I believe it is currently preserved as United Automobile BU2. Note the small wooden gate between neat hedges at the entrance to each house, before the trend started to pave the front garden and create a driveway to accommodate the family car.**

Above: **Another former ECW-bodied Bristol LS5G purchased at the same time as PHN 831 is also seen in Headstone Lane operating the 98B in July 1969. This is PHN 859, which had been new to United as its BU30 in March 1953.**

Below: **This is Elm Park Road in Pinner in July 1969, and working route 98B for Elms Coaches is VNO 869, an ECW-bodied Bristol LS5G new to Eastern National in February** 1953. It was originally fleet No 4200 and was a dual-purpose bus. The fleet number was changed to No 372 in July 1954, and the bus was converted to bus seats in November 1962. It was withdrawn in early 1965 and entered service with Daisy of Broughton in July of that year. The following year, via S. Twell of Ingham, it was purchased by Elm Coaches and entered service in November 1966.

Elmtree Transport

Route 98B (see the previous section) was handed on through a succession of private firms, including Atlas Coaches of Edgware. The operator working the service in 1975 was Elmtree Transport of Wealdstone.

An ECW-bodied Bristol LS6G, MAX 107, of Elmtree Transport is pictured at The Broadway, Hatch End, on 18 April 1975. This bus entered service with Red & White Service Ltd of Chepstow as its No U754 in June 1954.

During 1968 it was acquired by Crosville Motor Services Ltd, and remained with that company until 1973. It was purchased by Elmtree during the early part of 1975 and entered service in March, lasting a little over a year in service.

Golden Miller

red Varney's 'Golden Miller' business, with two coaches and a Twickenham booking office, was acquired in 1955 by F. G. Wilder & Sons Ltd of Feltham. It was rare in the 1950s for any regular bus service in London to be provided by an independent operator; the first such licence since the Second World War was granted to West London Coachways in October 1955 between Feltham station and Bedfont. This service was taken over by F. G. Wilder & Sons trading as Golden Miller, who numbered the route 601. On 1 January 1968 two further stage services were started, route 602 from Feltham to Shepperton Station, and the 603 to Hanworth. In November 1970 the Walton-on-Thames to Walton Station service of Walton on Thames Motor Co Ltd, which had begun in 1923 and was never taken over by the LPTB, was acquired by Golden Miller and extended to Oatlands Village, as route 604; however it was not a success and was withdrawn. The number 605 was intended for a route in the Claygate area, which never materialised, while the 606 was started in 1971, linking Staines town centre to Stanwell Moor and Stanwell Village, and separate from the rest of the Golden Miller network.

During 1961 Doncaster Corporation took delivery of six Roe-bodied AEC Reliances, Nos 25 to 30 (8625 DT to 8630 DT). This particular batch of buses did not have a long working life in Doncaster and all were withdrawn from service during 1970. Seen with Golden Miller at the Feltham Street terminus of route 601 in March 1972 is 8627 DT.

Right: **In the early 1960s Manchester Corporation was planning a future without double-deckers, so the days of the bus conductor would be numbered – at that time only a single-decker could be operated legally without one. As a preliminary step towards conversion to single-deck one-person operation, the Corporation carried out experiments in new methods of fare collection, initially using 20 Park Royal-bodied Panther Cubs, a model created by Leyland at Manchester's request. By the time another batch of 29 arrived in 1967, conductor-less operation of double-deck buses was fairly imminent, and Manchester's plan for an all-single-deck fleet was shelved. Between March and May 1965 a batch of 18 Park Royal-bodied Panther Cubs, Nos 63 to 80 (BND 863C to BND 880C), was delivered to Manchester Corporation. All were transferred to SELNEC in November 1969, but saw little or no service. Now working for Golden Miller and seen at the Feltham Station terminus of route 601 in May 1973 is BND 876C.**

Below: **In May 1960 Portsmouth Corporation took delivery of ten Weymann dual-doorway Leyland PSUC1/1s, Nos 16 to 25 (TTP 990 to 999). Photographed working the 601 service for Golden Miller on 18 April 1975 is TTP 997. The pedestrian footbridge next to the level crossing at Feltham station is just visible on the right. This turning circle and the adjacent land have since been redeveloped and buses now use a modern bus station next to the up-line station entrance, where cars can be seen parked beyond the optician's shop to the left of the picture.**

Hastings Tramway Company

The first trial trip of a tram in Hastings, with the Mayor on board, was on 15 July 1905, and it ran round the completed circular route in an anti-clockwise direction. There were 65 trams, all of the same double-deck canopy style with Dick Kerr bodies and Brill trucks, and they were numbered 1 to 65. Only 22 were ready for the opening day of the service on 31 July 1905, but they still managed to carry more than 18,000 passengers on the first day. By the mid-1920s the company had become interested in replacing the trams with trolleybuses, and an Act of 29 July 1927 gave Hastings Tramway the authority to run them. The first tramway to be replaced was the Hollington-Silverhill-Bohemia Road-Memorial line on 1 April 1928, and the last tramway, the rural St Helens-Baldslow-Silverhill line, was converted on 15 May 1929.

The trolleybuses purchased between 1928 and 1930 for tramway replacement comprised 58 Guy six-wheelers, of which

In 1939 Hastings Tramway ordered 48 new trolleybuses, the first 20 of which, AEC four-wheel double-deckers, entered service on 1 June 1940. The first ten, Nos 1 to 10 (BDY 776 to 785) were AEC 661Ts with bodywork by Weymann. This is No 7 (BDY 782) at the St Helens terminus on 10 September 1955. Of the 50 single-deckers replaced by the double-deckers, six (Nos 9, 18, 19, 24, 40 and 51) were sold to Nottingham Corporation in 1941, six (Nos 11, 13, 35, 38, 57 and one other) were sold to Derby Corporation in 1942, six (Nos 16, 29, 47, 48, 52 and 53) were acquired by Mexborough & Swinton Traction Co in 1943, and four (Nos 20, 45, 50 and 58) were retained by Hastings until 1955. Numbers 31, 33, 36 and 37 were scrapped in 1943, and the remainder were sold between 1943 and 1946. *David Clarke*

the first eight, Nos 1 to 8 (DY 4953, DY 4954 and DY 4965 to DY4970), were all open-top double-deckers with 57-seat bodies by Christopher Dodson Ltd. The remaining three batches, Nos 9 to 38 (DY 5111 to 5140), 39 to 48 (DY 5452 to 5461) and 49 to 58 (DY 5576 to 5585), were central-entrance single-deck 32-seaters with bodywork by Ransomes Sims & Jeffries Ltd. In 1935 Hastings Tramway Company was taken over by Maidstone & District.

Below: **The second batch of trolleybuses to enter service in June 1940 were Nos 11 to 20 (BDY 786 to BDY 795), AEC 661Ts with Park Royal bodywork. For many years the roofs of the trolleybuses were painted dark green, like the main panels, but later they became cream. In the peaceful suburb of Ore in September 1955 is No 14 (BDY 789).** *David Clarke*

Bottom: **The other order for 28 new trolleybuses was reduced to 25, and these did not arrive until after the war. The first batch, delivered in 1946, were Nos 21 to 30 (BDY 796 to BDY 805), and they were Sunbeams Ws with Weymann 56-seat bodywork. This is No 23 (BDY 798) descending the ramp leading from Harrow Bridge in September 1955.** *David Clarke*

Right: **At the Fishmarket, working the Circular Route 2, is another of the Park Royal-bodied Sunbeam Ws delivered in 1946, this time No 25 (BDY 800). After extensive research I have been unable to source any information on Theka Linctus; I can only presume that it was a locally produced cough mixture. On the closure of Hastings system on 31 May 1959 all the Park Royal-bodied Sunbeam Ws, Nos 21 to 30, were sold to Bradford City Transport for further service. Two of the Weymann-bodied Ws, BDY 815 and BDY 820, were also purchased by Bradford. All of these trolleybuses were withdrawn by Bradford by 1963.** *David Clarke*

Below: **The last batch of trolleybuses to be delivered to Hastings Tramways in 1948 were Nos 31 to 45 (BDY 806 to 820), and they were Sunbeam Ws with 56-seat Weymann bodywork. No 36 (BDY 811) is seen at East Beach on 10 September 1955 working route 11 to Hollington. Note that this is one of the trolleybuses that had a cream-painted roof. There is a wonderful selection of cars in the background, with, nearest the camera, a** Hillman Minx, a Morris Minor convertible, I think a Morris Oxford and, behind No 36, an Austin FX3 taxi cab. The FX3 was originally offered with a 2.2-litre petrol engine and an all-steel body by Carbodies. These popular taxis were produced between 1948 and 1958 and more than 7,000 were built. The Austin Motor Company developed a diesel engine and these became available for the FX3 in 1956. Most of the FX3s worked in the London area, but several hundred were in use in other parts of the UK. It was replaced by the FX4 in 1958, but soldiered on for many years. *David Clarke*

Above: **This is No 38 (BDY 813), another of the 1948 batch of Weymann-bodied Sunbeam Ws, at the Cooden terminus on 10 September 1955 – there's not a lot of passenger potential in this scene. A total of seven Hastings trolleybuses (BDY 806/808/812/813/814/816 and 819) were acquired by Walsall Corporation in 1959; they were given Walsall fleet numbers 303 to 310 respectively, and gave excellent service there. Five Hastings trolleybuses (Nos 32, 34, 35, 42 and 43) were acquired by Maidstone Corporation.** *David Clarke*

Below: **No 45 (BDY 820), numerically the last of the 1948 Weymann-bodied Sunbeam Ws, is seen in September 1955 in Queen's Road approaching the town centre. On 1 October 1957 Hastings Tramway Company was wound up and taken over by Maidstone & District Motor Services. The gold 'Hastings Tramways' fleet name disappeared fairly quickly from the trolleybuses, and in August 1958 it was announced that the trolleybus system would be ending and replaced by Leyland PDR1/1s. The system closed on the night of 31 May 1959, and trolleybus No 28 (BDY 803) made the final journey to Silverhill depot.** *David Clarke*

London Country

The London Passenger Transport Board (LPTB) was set up by the London Passenger Transport Act of 13 April 1933, and came into being on 1 July, covering the so-called London Passenger Transport Area. The LPTA had an approximate radius of 30 miles from Charing Cross to Baldock in the north, Brentwood in the east, Horsham in the south and High Wycombe in the west. A total of 92 undertakings came under the authority of the LPTB. The Central area buses, trams and trolleybuses were painted red, and the coaches and Country buses green, with coaches being the Green Line. The Country bus and coach department took charge of the Country area and the Green Line coach operation, which comprised 66 independent operators and 246 routes. The LPTB was replaced by the London Transport Executive in 1948 under the Transport Act of 1947.

During the 1950s London Country became dominated by AEC Regent and Regal buses, with a small number of Guy Vixens for lightly loaded rural routes. From the mid-1950s the department was occupied by the transport provision for the new towns of Crawley, Harlow, Hatfield, Hemel Hempstead, Stevenage and Welwyn Garden City.

From 1 January 1970 London Country Bus Services was formed as part of the National Bus Company, and took over an old, clapped-out and unsuitable fleet of buses.

In October 1954 seven of the early pre-war RTs, RT 36/62/79/93/114/128 and 137, were overhauled and given a new lease of life. Repainted in green and cream and with their displays restored, except for the rear 'To' box, they were transferred to Hertford in May 1955 to replace STLs on route 327 between Nazeing Gate and Broxbourne – a weak bridge prevented the use of the heavier post-war RTs. This is RT 36 (FXT 211) on 10 December 1955. This bus was withdrawn in February 1963 and had been sold by April 1963. *David Clarke*

Above: **The seven RTs worked route 327 until August 1957, when they were stored at Potters Bar, then became trainers, some with the Country area, and some in the Central area, all retaining their green livery. This is RT 137 (FXT 312) at Broxbourne station on 27 July 1957, just a few days before the pre-war RTs were withdrawn from the route and stored. The bus became a trainer at Reigate, remaining there until March 1963, and was sold for scrap later that year.** *David Clarke*

Right: **This is RT 986 (JXN 14), an AEC Regent III that, when new, had a Weymann RT10 body with roofbox. It entered service from Hertford in October 1948 on route 310A and stayed there until 1957, when it was transferred to Dartford. From January 1961 until October 1971 it worked from Hatfield, Leatherhead and St Albans depots. Between October 1971 and June 1976, apart from a couple of short breaks, it worked from Chelsham depot. RT 986 is seen working route 403 in Croydon on 23 September 1975. It was transferred to Godstone in June 1976, withdrawn in February 1977 and sold for scrap in June of that year. Route 403 began running on 16 August 1921**

as London General's route S3 between West Croydon and Sevenoaks; it was renumbered 403 on 1 December 1924. By the mid-1970s the route ran between Wallington and Chesham with an extension to Warlingham Park Hospital. Route 403 had Chelsham's biggest allocation of buses and was one of the busiest services on the south side of the Thames. It also had the distinction of being the last London Country route to be operated by RTs.

Right: **This is RT 1418 (JXC 181), a Craven's roofbox-bodied AEC Regent III new in March 1949. It entered service in March 1949 from Windsor depot and spent most of its service life there. This view was taken at Uxbridge station in July 1955. The bus was withdrawn from service in March 1956 and sold to Birds of Stratford-upon-Avon in May 1956. Lowland Motorways of Glasgow purchased it in June 1956 and RT 1418 entered service the next month. It passed to Scottish Omnibuses on the takeover of Lowland Motorways in January 1958, was numbered BB 1 and remained in service until it was withdrawn in early 1963 and sold for scrap in May. Route 457 ran from Windsor bus station to Uxbridge through Iver Heath, George Green and Slough.** *David Clarke*

Right: **The first 20 Weymann lowbridge-bodied AEC Regent IIIs, Nos RLH 1 to 20 (KYY 501 to 520), were delivered between May and August 1950. They were of the RLH1 type, with roof ventilators and added trafficators (including RM-type indicators on the rear panel). These buses had the front numberplates mounted originally below the chromed radiators, roll-up radiator blinds and no rear-wheel discs. The route stencil holder on the rear window fell out of use early on. All were originally green, with some repainted later. A total of six were allocated to Godstone, six went to Amersham and eight to Addlestone for the Staines routes 436, 436A, 461, 461A and 463. Number RLH 1 (KYY 501) was allocated to Amersham for route 336, and this view of it was taken** on its first day in service, seemingly having problems. During 1956 RLH 1 was overhauled, repainted red and transferred to Harrow Weald depot for route 230. In 1959 it was transferred to Dalston for route 178, then by February 1962 was working routes 248A and 249 from Romford depot. It was withdrawn in December 1964, and after working as a staff bus with Gliksten & Sons, was scrapped in December 1969. *David Clarke*

Above: This is RT 2722 (LYR 706), an AEC Regent III with Park Royal bodywork, new in October 1951. The bus entered service in January 1952 from Peckham and stayed there until 1957, when it was transferred for a couple of years to Hendon and, from October 1959 until September 1963, Holloway depot. Transferred in that month to London Country's Hertford depot, it worked there until October 1968. Between then and August 1973 it worked out of St Albans, Reigate, Hertford and Crawley depots, eventually ending its travels at Windsor. On 18 April 1975 RT 2722 is seen in Thames Street, Windsor, working route 452 from Windsor Bus Station to Uxbridge Station. This bus was withdrawn from service eight months later and sold for scrap in March 1976.

Right: This is a very rare view of RT 3251 (LLU 610), a Weymann-bodied AEC Regent III, at Chalk Farm depot, just delivered in early August 1950. The bus entered service from Romford depot and worked

services 721, 722 and 726. It stayed at Romford until mid-1965, then until mid-1972 saw service at High Wycombe and Leatherhead. In September 1972 it was purchased by the London Transport Executive, saw service at Catford, Bromley, Bexleyheath and Barking, and was used on the final run of the RT in Barking in April 1979. *David Clarke*

Right: In 1952 Guy produced chassis for 84 buses, which received ECW bodywork, and by agreement with the licensing authority they seated 26, but were still allowed to be single-manned. Sliding ventilators were fitted to the windows rather than the standard wind-down type. They were powered by a Perkins P6 diesel engine and entered service between October 1953 and January 1954. This is GX 58 (MXX 358), which entered service in December 1953 and was allocated to East Grinstead to work on service 494 between there and Oxted, with some journeys continuing to Limpsfield and Chart Church. GS 58 and GS 59 were the East Grinstead-based Guys, and GS 58 stayed there until August 1962, when GS 39 took over. GS 58 was then allocated to Northfleet and remained there until its withdrawal in May 1967; it was subsequently sold to the National Trust at Lapworth. *David Clarke*

Below: Route 301 was one of the Country area's major trunk services and ran between Watford Heath and Aylesbury via Watford, Huntonbridge, King's Langley, Apsley Mills, Two Waters, Hemel Hempstead, Boxmoor, Berkhamsted, Northchurch and Tring. Working the 301 route from Aylesbury in August 1969 is RT 4344 (NLP 509), a Park Royal-bodied AEC Regent III.

Right: **Route 384 ran between Hertford Bus Station and Letchworth Station. On leaving Hertford it headed east to Ware, then on through the villages of Tonwell, Sacombe, Dane End, Whempstead, Benington and Walkern before reaching Stevenage bus station via Pin Green. The route then continued to Letchworth via Graveley and Wilian. It was cut back to Stevenage in the 1970s. Working route 384 in Stevenage on 20 July 1974 is RF 49 (LYF 400), an**

AEC Regal IV with Metro-Cammell bodywork. It was new in December 1951 and worked from Reigate depot until 1957. It transferred to Luton in 1957, then to Hemel Hempstead in April 1959. In April 1963 it was stored for a period before being used on route 720 from Harlow depot. It was modernised in November 1966 and transferred to Tring, where it remained until 1972. By April 1974 RF 49 was working out of Hertford depot until its withdrawal in July 1975. It was sold for scrap in November 1975.

Below: **Working route 364 in Luton in July 1972 is Metro-Cammell-bodied AEC Regal IV RF 265 (MLL 802). This bus was new to Swanley depot in June 1952 and worked there until February 1960. From then until April 1964 it worked from Chelsham depot. Transferred to St. Albans in April 1964, RF 265 was downgraded to a bus in January 1967, and remained in St Albans until March 1971, when it was transferred to Luton for the remainder of its service life. Withdrawn from service in February 1974, it had been sold by April. Route 364 ran daily between Luton and**

Flamstead Village via Farley Hill, Woodside, Markyate and Friars Wash. There was a Monday to Saturday extension from Luton to Hitchin via Cockernhoe, Tea Green, The Heath, Breachwood Green, Kings Walden, Preston and Gosmore. The route was operated by Hitchin garage until it closed in 1958, when Luton took on the duties, and extended the service to Markyate and Flamstead. The service gradually declined, and was withdrawn in 1972 as part of London Country's rural cutbacks of that year.

Above: Route 425 ran daily between Guildford and Dorking through the picturesque villages of Shalford, Chilworth, Albury, Shere Gomshall, Abinger Hammer, Wotton and Westcott. Seen in Albury in September 1971 is Metro-Cammell-bodied AEC Regal IV RF 599 (NLE 599). New to Reigate in October 1957, it remained there until April 1958, when it was transferred to Hemel Hempstead. It was converted to one-person operation in August 1958 and transferred to Garston, then Dorking, where it remained until November 1966. Guildford was the next destination, where it remained until September 1972, finishing its service life at Hertford. RF 599 was withdrawn in January 1975 and had been sold by April of that year.

were withdrawn in 1972, and in 1974 the route was diverted in Welwyn Garden City from Valley Road to Lemsford Lane. Working route 330 in Hemel Hempstead on 20 July 1974 is RMC 1456 (456 CLT), a Park Royal-bodied AEC Routemaster. This bus, together with another 19 RMCs in August 1962, was initially allocated to Guildford to work on route 715/715A between Hertford/Guildford and Marble Arch. In April 1967 RMC 1456 went for overhaul and was then allocated to Windsor, then Hemel Hempstead to work on route 330. In June 1979 it was sold to London Transport for conversion to a trainer, then in March 1989 it was fully refurbished for use on the X15.

Right: In 1950 route 330 ran daily between St Albans and Welwyn Garden City via Oaklands, Smallford, New Hatfield, Stanborough and Valley Road. In the late 1950s it was extended from St Albans to Hemel Hempstead via Leverstock Green, and beyond Welwyn Garden City, with buses running to either Howlands or Great Ganett. The Great Ganett journeys

Right: **Route 405 ran between West Croydon and Crawley bus stations through South Croydon, Purley, Coulsdon, Hooley, Merstham, Redhill, Earlswood, Salfords, Horley, Gatwick Airport, Lowfield Heath and County Oak. Seen in Horley on 24 September 1975 working service 405 to Crawley is RCL 2221 (CUV 221C), a Park Royal-bodied AEC Routemaster. This bus originally was a 30-foot coach with an 11.3-litre AEC AV690 engine and a semi-automatic gear change with high-ratio gearing. New in May 1965, in June it entered service on routes 721, 722 and 726 from Romford depot. Downgraded to a bus in early 1972, it was transferred to Reigate. In March 1978 London Transport purchased the bus and by January 1979 it had been converted to an exhibition bus.**

Below: **Route 709 was introduced in 1946 and initially ran from Caterham to Baker Street through Old Coulsdon, Coulsdon, Purley, South Croydon, West Croydon, Thornton Heath Pond, Norbury, Streatham, Brixton, Kennington, Trafalgar Square and Oxford Circus. It was extended north-west to Chesham through Notting Hill Gate, Shepherds Bush, North Acton, Northolt, Uxbridge, Denham, Gerrards Cross, Chalfont St Peter, Chalfont St Giles and Amersham,** and south from Caterham to Godstone. In 1965, however, it was cut back to Baker Street again, then ran daily between Godstone Garage and Oxford Circus, continuing on to Chesham on weekdays. Route 709 was the last Green Line route to use crew operation, with RCL Class long Routemaster coaches, providing just three return journeys during Monday to Friday peak hours, and one return journey on Sundays between Godstone and Baker Street. Working a peak-hour 709 in Old Coulsdon on 24 September 1975 is RCL 2250 (CUV 250C). This bus was first allocated to Grays in July 1965, then transferred to Dunton Green in December 1967 to work on routes 704 and 705. By November 1968 it was working out of Godstone garage, and during May 1976 was demoted to a bus. Returning to Grays in October 1978, it had the distinction of making the last London Country RCL journey when it ran a school special in Grays on 24 January 1979. It was purchased by London Transport in March 1979, and converted to an open top in 1991.

Top: **Seen in Croydon on 7 January 1978 is RML 2330 (CUV 330C), a Park Royal-bodied AEC Routemaster. New in October 1965, it was put into service from Godstone depot on routes 409 to 411, and spent all of its London Country service life there. During July 1979 it was sold to London Transport, which did not withdraw it until September 2004. Route 411 ran daily from West Croydon bus station to Reigate through South Croydon, Purley, Old Coulsdon, Caterham-on-the-Hill, Caterham, Godstone, Bletchingley, Nunfield and Redhill.**

Middle: **Route 347 ran daily between Uxbridge Station and Garston Garage through Denham, Harefield, Mount Vernon Hospital, Northwood, Oxhey, Bushey and Watford; it was extended on Mondays to Saturdays to Hemel Hempstead bus station through Abbots Langley, Bedmond and Leverstock Green. Working the route on 20 July 1974 is RML 2419 (JJD 419D), a Park Royal-bodied AEC Routemaster. First allocated to High Wycombe in February 1966, it was quickly transferred to Grays, where it spent most of its service life with London Country. In December 1977 it was purchased by London Transport and was in service between January 1978 and early 2004.**

Bottom: **Eleven Metro-Cammell dual-door-bodied AEC Merlins with 11.3-litre AEC AH691 diesel engines, seating 25 with 48 standees, entered service on the Hemel Hempstead town services 314A/B/C in February 1969. Working service 314A on 20 July 1974 is MBS 288 (VLW 288G), allocated to Hemel Hempstead from February 1969 to February 1975, during which time it was re-seated to 32, then 33. From February 1975 to January 1977 it worked out of Grays depot, then returned to Hemel Hempstead. Withdrawn from service in March 1979, it was sold for scrap in February 1980. The car in the background is a Vauxhall Cresta PC, first introduced at the London Motor Show in October 1965. A total of 53,912 were produced between 1965 and 1972.**

Above: **Route 463 originally ran daily between Woking and Walton-on-Thames through Woodham, New Haw, Addlestone and Weybridge. By 1952 it had been extended from Woking to Guildford bus station through Kingfield Green, Old Woking, Send, Burnt Common, Clandon, West Clandon and Merrow. Working the route in Walton-on-Thames in March 1972 is SM 140 (BPH 140H), a Park Royal-bodied AEC Swift. New in August 1970, it was allocated to Guildford and worked from there until May 1974, when it was transferred to Addlestone, remaining there until August 1977. Transferred to Windsor, it became a driver trainer until withdrawal in September 1980. Fitted with an 8.2-litre diesel engine, this class of buses was underpowered and tended to be unreliable; they were withdrawn after relatively short service lives. SM 140 was sold for scrap in July 1981.**

Right: **In October and November 1970 a free demonstration service called 'Better Buses for Stevenage' was operated by SM 146 and SM 147, Metro-Scania single-deckers from Leicester Corporation, and a demonstrator with London Transport, VWD 451H. When new one-person-operated buses were put onto the Stevenage bus station to Chells service in March 1971, there were problems with headway and fare collecting. On 20 May 1971 London Country**

introduced a farebox, and by the end of July Stevenage 'Superbus' was up and running. The livery chosen was a canary yellow with blue relief. The first buses on the route were five SMs with two MSs, and from 12 February 1972 another two MSs were allocated. Two more SMs were added in March 1972, and a further two in April. On 2 September 1972 a new Superbus route was introduced, SB2, which ran from the bus station to St Nicholas. Working this service on 20 July 1974 is SM 482 (DPD 482J), a Metro-Cammell dual-doorway-bodied AEC Swift. It was first allocated to Stevenage for service 809, but later transferred to Leatherhead before returning to Stevenage in February 1972 to take up Superbus duties. In April 1976 it was repainted NBC green and worked from Dunton Green and finally Windsor. It was withdrawn in February 1978 and sold by October 1978.

Above: Route 446 ran daily between Slough Station and Farnham Road via Whitby Road, and in later years, as seen here, it became a circular to Wexham Park Hospital. Seen in Slough on 10 July 1978 is SM 515 (DPD 515J), a Metro-Cammell-bodied AEC Swift that began its service life in Chesham. Within two months it was transferred to Dartford, where it remained until October 1972. Transferred to Harlow until March 1975, from then until its withdrawal in March 1979 it was allocated to Windsor depot. Malta and Belfast were two places where many ex-London Transport AEC Swifts found good homes, and gave good service.

Right: South Wales Transport ordered 21 AEC Swifts with Alexander dual-purpose bodies for delivery in early 1972, but the order was diverted to London Country and the buses began to arrive in January 1972. They had 8.3-litre engines and the Alexander bodywork featured deep

windows of two heights, which gave an excellent view for the passengers. The whole batch went into service on route 725, which included several hilly sections in Bromley and Chislehurst, where the engines were found wanting. After just over six years on route 725 the SMAs were worn out and scrapped. Working the 725 at Windsor bus station on 18 April 1975 is SMA 14 (JPF 114K), which was allocated new to Dartford in March 1972 and remained there for the whole of its service life.

Right: **Route 716 was introduced in 1946 and ran from Chertsey to Hitchin through Addlestone, Weybridge, Walton, East Molesey, Hampton Court, Kingston, Ham, Richmond, Barnes, Hammersmith, Kensington, Hyde Park Corner, Marble Arch, Baker Street, Finchley Road, Golders Green, North Finchley, Barnet, Potters Bar, Brookmans Park, Hatfield, Welwyn Garden City, Knebworth and Stevenage. Operated throughout most of the 1950s and early 1960s by AEC Regal RF coaches, conversion to RMC Routemaster coaches came in 1963. The route reverted to one-person-operation single-deckers in 1972, and was merged with the 716A, the southern terminus switching to Woking. In 1978 it was withdrawn north of Oxford Circus, with the southern section not surviving much longer. At Stevenage bus station on 20 July 1974 is RP 52 (JPA 152K), a Park Royal coach-seated AEC Reliance that entered service from Addlestone in February 1972. These buses had 11.3-litre diesel engines and were first put into service on route 727 in December 1971. RP 52 replaced an RMC on route 716 in March 1972 and remained at Addlestone for its entire London Country service life.**

Below: **This excellent view shows AN 5 (JPL 105K), a dual-doorway Park Royal-bodied Leyland PDR1A/1 in Bletchingly on 24 September 1975. This bus was part of a large batch delivered to London Country between March and October 1972. The first 16 were** initially allocated to Hertford to convert route 310 and 310A from Hertford to Enfield from RT operation, but apparently they were not as reliable as the buses they replaced. AN 5 was quickly transferred to Stevenage, and was there until December 1976. From then until it sale in January 1995 it had a long service and trainer history. In 2007 it was acquired by Emblings of Guyhirn for spares. The cars parked to the right are a Ford Granada Mark I and a Skoda. The former was produced between 1972 and 1977, at Koln and Dagenham from 1972 until 1976, when production switched entirely to Germany. The Skoda is a 100/110 model, produced by Skoda Auto in Czechoslovakia between 1969 and 1976; well over 1,100,000 were produced.

Top: **In July 1971 London Country purchased two dual-doorway Metro-Scania BR111s, MS 1 and 2 (GPB 19J and 20J), with 45 seats, and they entered service on the Stevenage 'Superbus' routes in July 1971. Two more, MS 3 and 4 (JPH 68K and 69K), were purchased in April 1972; these were Metro-Scania CR111MHs, and also entered service on the Superbus routes. Working SB2 on 20 July 1974 is MS 4 (JPH 69K); it was withdrawn in November 1978 and gathered dust at Radlett Airfield until sold for scrap in August 1980.**

Middle: **During 1971 King Alfred took delivery of its last new buses, AOU 108K to AOU 110K, dual-doorway Metro-Scanias with 47 seats. In 1973 they were swapped with Hants & Dorset, who had purchased King Alfred, for three Leyland Nationals, which were all reduced to 45 seats, repainted in Stevenage 'Superbus' livery and entered service in January 1974. Seen six months later working route SB2 is MS 6 (AOU 109J). This bus was withdrawn in January 1978, and in August 1980, like all the London Country Metro-Scanias, was sold for scrap.**

Bottom: **London Country was among the first NBC companies to purchase Leyland Nationals, the first being standard dual-doorway 37-foot buses. The first, LN 1 (KPA 101K), arrived in Reigate in mid-April 1972 and was painted all-over yellow – British Leyland would only paint buses in one colour. The bus had defects and was returned to Workington; on returning to Reigate, it received blue window surrounds and the 'SB' logo. The first two started work on the 'Superbus' on 9 September 1972, followed by two more L-registered Nationals in December 1972. LN 1 is seen working route SB1 in July 1974. It remained at Stevenage until early 1979 when it went to Crawley works and re-emerged as a trainer from Reigate depot in May 1981. From January 1983 it remained in store, apart from limited use as a mobile classroom, and was scrapped by July 1986.**

London Transport

Prior to 1933, the ownership and management of the transport system in London was distributed among a large number of independent and separate organisations. The tram and trolleybus network was owned by various local authorities and public companies, and buses were also owned by numerous companies. London County Council managed the tram operations within the County of London, but its responsibility did not extend to tram or bus services outwith the county. The London Passenger Transport Act of 1933 set up the London Passenger Transport Board to unify transport services in the London area. From 1 July 1933 the Act removed responsibility for 167.17 miles of tram routes from the LCC, three county boroughs and a number of local authorities, and the supervision of buses were taken over from the Metropolitan Police. The area taken over was known as the London Passenger Transport Area.

From 1 January 1948 London Transport was taken into public ownership as the London Transport Executive, part of the British Transport Commission. During this period of management, the AEC Routemaster was introduced in 1956, and this period also saw the withdrawal of trams in 1952 and trolleybuses in 1962. From the 1 January 1963 the London Transport Board was the transport authority, and reported directly to the Minister of Transport. During this time there was little investment in public transport in London.

Legislation creating the Greater London Council was passed in 1963, and the GLC became the transport authority from 1 January 1970 until 28 June 1984. The GLC broadly controlled transport within the Greater London boundary. The Country buses and Green Line coaches passed to London Country Bus Services, which in 1970 became part of the National Bus Company.

This is the junction of St Georges Road and Westminster Bridge Road on 4 April 1952, and working route 35 is ex-Leyton tram No 175. Built during 1931, it was scrapped in December 1952. It is advertising Bisto, whose very first product, in 1908, was a meat-flavoured gravy powder, which rapidly became a bestseller in the UK. Invented by Messrs Roberts & Patterson, it was named 'Bisto' because it 'browns, seasons and thickens in one'. *David Clarke*

Above: Working route 78 to Victoria Station on 1 January 1952 is ex-Leyton tram No 177, built in 1931. This view was taken at Stockwell Underground station only a few months before the tram was scrapped in June 1952. It is advertising 'The Ale of Pubs – Watneys'. Watneys began brewing in the 19th century at the Stag Brewery in Pimlico, and went through a number of mergers, becoming Watney, Combe & Reid in 1898, Watney Mann in 1958, and finally merging with Grand Metropolitan Hotels in 1972. Watney Mann was closed in 1979, but when you are walking around London there is still evidence that some pubs were part of Watney's estate. *David Clarke*

Right: Ex-Leyton Class E3 tram No 198 was new in 1931 and scrapped in May 1952. This is Brixton on 1 January 1952, and the tram is on route 78 to West Norwood. Trams to Croydon went past Smarts the furnishers, and the van in front of the store is delivering Hornimans Tea. John Horniman started a tea merchants business in 1826, with a warehouse just north of the City in Shepherdess Walk. The story is that he was one of the first merchants to have the idea of selling tea in packets. The firm prospered and advertised widely, so that Horniman's tea became a household name. In 1918 the company was bought out by J. Lyons, but the name lived on and Horniman's tea was still available in the USA until the mid-1990s. *David Clarke*

Right: **This excellent view is of Lewisham High Street on 28 December 1951. The bus working route 108 between Poplar, Eltham, Woolwich or Crystal Palace through the Blackwall Tunnel is STL 1830 (DLU 196). The Blackwall Tunnel had a small bore and some sharp bends, requiring special buses. A total of 40 STLs were delivered during March and April 1937 with roofs to a special profile and tapered rear ends. At times they also appeared on route 82 through the Rotherhithe Tunnel. They spent almost all their time at Athol Street depot in Poplar, and only when the Blackwall Tunnel was altered in 1953 did this batch of special STLs lose its monopoly on route 108. STL 1830 was withdrawn from service in April 1953, and the last of the batch went in early 1954. The Green Line RF is one of the batch with LYF 3xx registrations, which entered service from Windsor, Tunbridge Wells and Reigate between October and December 1951. The tram working route 54 between Grove Park Station and Victoria Station is ex-Croydon No 388, built in 1927 and scrapped in March 1952.** *David Clarke*

Below: **This is Stanstead Road, Blythe Vale, in the South East London suburbs on 27 December 1951, and working route 74 to Grove Park is E1 tram No 571. This tram was built in 1930 using trucks and electrical components from an ex-G Class single-decker. It was scrapped in April 1952.** *David Clarke*

Right: Working route 54 to Victoria on 28 December 1951 is tram No 575, an example of the final style of E1 body placed on Class G single-deckers. This view was taken at Lewisham Obelisk, and in the background are a re-built E1 and an RTL. This tram was scrapped by March 1952. *David Clarke*

Below: This is Lewisham High Road at the junction of St Donetts Road on 23 June 1952, and working route 46 from Woolwich to the City is tram No 577, an E1 built in 1930. This tram was built using trucks from Class G single-deckers, and they are recognisable by the thick centre pillar of the lower saloon. This tram was in service from Abbey Road on route 36 on the last day of trams in London, 5 July 1952, and was scrapped in September of that year. Heading towards the camera is an RT working route 179, a tram replacement route that started on 6 January 1952 between Grove Park and Farringdon Street; it was withdrawn on 8 November 1961 and replaced by route 141 and 141A. *David Clarke*

Above: **This view was taken at New Cross depot on 28 December 1951. The car in the centre is an HR2 no-trolley conduit tramcar, which were numbered 101 to 159, 512 to 544, and 726 and 160. London had a hybrid network of double-deck trams, where overhead collection was used in the outer sections and conduit in the centre. The change-over process from conduit to overhead wire was largely automatic: the conductor released the trolley pole onto the wire then, as the tram moved forward, the conduit channel veered sideways to outside the running track, automatically ejecting the collector plough – the tram was said to be 'shooting the plough'. At the change-over between overhead wire and conduit, the process was a little more complicated. The tram pulled up alongside a ploughman who engaged a two-pronged guide, known as a 'plough fork', over the plough in a short length of unelectrified conduit which led into the plough channel beneath the centre of the tram. As the tram drew forward, the conduit channel moved beneath the tram, carrying the plough into position. The conductor could then pull down the trolley pole and stow it. Building conduit tramways was an expensive option, so the more suburban areas used the overhead wire arrangement.**

'Hovis', being advertised by the tram on the left, was named by a London student, Herbert Grime, in a national competition set by S. Fitton & Sons Ltd to find a trading name for its flour, which was rich in wheat germ. He won £25 when he coined the word from the Latin phrase 'hominis vis' – 'the strength of man'. The Hovis process was patented on 6 October 1887 by Richard Smith, and S. Fitton & Sons Ltd developed the brand, milling the flour and selling it together with Hovis branded baking tins to other bakers. **The firm became Hovis Limited in 1918.** *David Clarke*

Below: **This view was also taken outside New Cross depot, this time during August 1950. Nearest the camera is No 982, built in 1907 and rehabilitated in May 1935. The other trams in view are a previous rebuild of an E1 and, behind it, No 982, an unrebuilt E1.** *David Clarke*

Right: **Working route 35 to Kingsway Subway on 31 March 1952 is LCC E3 tram No 1908. This view was taken at the Nag's Head at Holloway, and on the left is a Lyons van. J. Lyons & Co was founded in 1887, and was best known for its chain of tea shops, which began in 1894 at 213 Piccadilly, peaked at around 250, but all had disappeared by 1981. Swiss rolls – rolled sponge cakes – were probably one of Lyons' most famous cakes, and were available as vanilla-filled chocolate sponge, chocolate-filled plain sponge, and plain sponge filled with lemon curd, greengage, raspberry, apricot, strawberry, nut and vanilla, cherry and vanilla, or almond. On 28 July 1978 Allied Breweries offered to buy the company, and just over a month later the terms of the sale were agreed and the name only survived for a few more years.** *David Clarke*

Right: **This is No 1962, an E3 tram, working route 35 at Camberwell Church Street on 4 April 1952. I think the lorry is an Austin K2/K4 series I.** *David Clarke*

Above: **Also working route 35, at Walworth Road on 4 April 1952, is E3 tram No 1979. The advert on the side is for Saxa Salt, a brand launched in 1907 by the Cerebos Company, which already produced a range of salt products, the majority of which were sold in bulk. Saxa's new, handy-sized packets were more convenient, and could be placed straight onto the table. Salt is relatively cheap and easy to get hold of today, but for thousands of years it was a highly valued commodity, and was even used as a method of payment. An effective food preservative, it was also believed to have healing properties. It was this belief in its medicinal value that, in 1894, led chemist George Weddell, founder of the Cerebos Company, to create the type of salt we use today. Weddell's daughter had been very ill, but during that era tablets containing vitamins or trace elements to supplement the diet were not available. As a chemist, Weddell knew that magnesium carbonate and calcium phosphate could strengthen his daughter's teeth and bones, so he mixed small quantities of both with salt, and the result was a free-running grain that, unlike the old-fashioned, coarse blocks, did not have to be crushed in order to be placed in salt cellars. Weddell began manufacturing his new product, which sold extremely well and was awarded a Royal warrant. As well as Saxa, the Cerebos Company created other classic brands such as Bisto, before being acquired in the 1960s by grocery group RHM.** *David Clarke*

Above: A total of 199 Chiswick-bodied AEC Renowns, Nos LT 1001 to 1036 and LT 1038 to 1200, were produced between December 1930 and December 1931. The first, LT 1001, entered service from Edgware depot on route 104. The 'Scooters', as they became known, were distributed widely throughout London. This is LT 1080 (GO 7151) at Archway Tavern in August 1950. It entered service from Sutton depot in June 1931, and in May 1950 was fitted with a diesel engine. By 1952 it was working from Hounslow depot, and was withdrawn from service in December 1952. *David Clarke*

Below: LT 1131 (GP 3407) was another Chiswick-bodied AEC Renown, which entered service from Leyton depot in June 1931. During the war the bus was badly damaged, and from August 1944 was rebuilt by Twiddy & Son of Norwich. The rebuild included a flatter roof, raised front destination box, square cab and perimeter seating. The bus re-entered service in February 1945 and worked from Sidcup, Muswell Hill, Leyton and Bromley depots. By 1950 it was working out of Sutton depot on service 212, and is captured on this service at Finsbury Park station in August 1950. It was withdrawn in October 1952 and sold to Morgan of Newport in February 1953. *David Clarke*

Right: **The 'leaning back' STLs, totalling 400 buses (STL 203 to 552 and STL 559 to 608), were produced between August 1933 and November 1934. The last batch, STL 559 to 608, entered service between October and November 1934, were fitted with second-hand petrol engines, and had Daimler pre-selector gearboxes and fluid flywheels. The whole batch were converted to diesel engines (A173 7.7-litre direct injection) during 1939. At Camden Town terminus in August 1950 is STL 606 (AYV 757), which entered service from Catford depot in November 1934 and was there until May 1939, when it was converted to diesel and transferred to Chalk Farm, where It remalned until its withdrawal from service two months after this photograph was taken.** *David Clarke*

Below: **Chiswick built a batch of roofbox STLs, STL 2189 to 2515, between June 1937 and March 1938, 94 of which were fitted with steel floors, while the remainder had wooden floors. This is STL 2323 (EGO 379), which entered service in October 1937 from Camberwell depot and was not withdrawn until December 1950. This view was taken at the Archway Tavern in August 1950.** *David Clarke*

Top: **Passing Carshalton depot on 1 October 1955 is trolleybus No 87 (CGF 87), a B1 Class Leyland with BRCW bodywork that was new in January 1936. Formerly named Sutton trolleybus depot, it was renamed Carshalton in 1950. The last day of operation of trolleybuses was 3 March 1959, and two bus routes took over the next day, route 154 between Morden and Crystal Palace and route 157 between Raynes Park and Crystal Palace. Trolleybus No 87 was withdrawn in March 1959 and Carshalton depot closed in 1964.** *David Clarke*

Middle: **Crossing the junction of Carshalton Road and Park Hill is trolleybus No 88 (CGF 88), another of the B1 Class Leylands with BRCW bodywork, new in January 1936; it was withdrawn at the end of trolleybus operation from Carshalton depot in March 1959. The car is either an A40 or A50, which were introduced in September 1954 and had identical bodywork. The A40 had a 1.2-litre straight four engine, whereas the A50 had a new 1.5-litre engine. A new A50 in 1955 cost £720 including taxes.** *David Clarke*

Bottom: **This is Anerley Hill at Crystal Palace Low Level station on 10 March 1956. The driver of trolleybus No 92 (CGF 92) has already turned his destination screen, no doubt eager to get back to Carshalton depot and off! The trolleybus is a Class B1 Leyland with a Birmingham Railway & Carriage Works body, which entered service in January 1936 and was withdrawn and scrapped in March 1959.** *David Clarke*

Top: **Working route 654 to Sutton at Reeve's Corner in West Croydon on 1 October 1955 is No 93 (CGF 93), a B1 Class BRCW-bodied Leyland that entered service in January 1936 and was withdrawn and scrapped in March 1959. The car heading away from the camera with registration JVB 523 is a Ford Anglia E494A, which was a very spartan car, and was the lowest priced four-wheeled car in 1948. It took more than 38 seconds to get to 50mph, but if you had £309 in your wallet you could be the proud owner of a brand new Ford Anglia.** *David Clarke*

Middle: **This is Harlesden Clock Tower in June 1955, and working route 660 to Hammersmith is No 188 (CUL 188). This C2 Class AEC 664T with Metro Cammell bodywork was new in March 1936 and withdrawn in June 1958. Note the wonderful white-walled tyres of the Ford on the left.** *David Clarke*

Bottom: **This is the junction of Goldhawk Road and Padderwick Road on 8 August 1956, and working route 660 from North Finchley to Hammersmith is No 279 (CUL 279), another C2 with Metro-Cammell bodywork, new in August 1936 and withdrawn in November 1959.** *David Clarke*

Above: Passing Willesden Green station in June 1955 is No 292 (CUL 292), a Class C3 AEC 664T with BRCW bodywork, which entered service in May 1936 and was withdrawn in August 1959. The car is a Jaguar Mark IV, with a 2,664cc engine sourced from Standard, but with the cylinder head reworked by SS Cars Ltd to give 105bhp. Between 1935 and 1948 6,281 cars of this marque were made. Willesden Green station opened on 24 November 1879, and the main station buildings, which date from the reconstruction of 1925, are fine examples of the work of C. W. Clark, the Metropolitan Railway's architect. The station became a Grade 2 listed building in December 2006. *David Clarke*

Below: Unfortunately I cannot make out the name on the side of the horse-drawn milk float, so we will call him Ernie, with the fastest milk float in Cricklewood Lane! Working route 645 to Barnet in June 1955 is No 311 (CUL 311), another C3 Class AEC 664T with BRCW bodywork, which was new in July 1936 and retired in August 1959. The car is, I think, a Jaguar Mark IV, but I am intrigued by the person by the traffic lights – St John Ambulance is my guess! *David Clarke*

Above: This is Golders Green in the late summer of 1955, and working route 660 is No 359 (CUL 359), a C3 Class AEC 664T new in August 1936 and withdrawn in November 1959. The Midland Bank was one of the big four banking groups in the UK for most of the 20th century, and is now part of HSBC. It was founded as the Birmingham & Midland Bank in Union Street, Birmingham, in August 1836, and expanded to absorb many local Midlands banks. In 1891 it merged with the Central Bank of London Ltd, becoming the London City & Midland Bank. After a period of nationwide expansion, including the acquisition of many smaller banks, the name Midland Bank Ltd was adopted in 1923, and by 1934 it was the largest deposit bank in the world. In 1992 HSBC Holdings plc acquired full ownership, and it was renamed HSBC bank in 1999. *David Clarke*

Below: This is Dartford, at the eastern extremity of the London trolleybus system, on 12 March 1955. About to depart on route 696 to Woolwich Ferry is No 395 (DGY 395), a D2 Class all-Leyland that was new in November 1936. It was withdrawn after the last day of service of route 696, 3 March 1959, and scrapped a month later. *David Clarke*

Above: **No 492 (DGY 492), a B1 Class Leyland with BRCW bodywork, was one of the shorter-wheelbase trolleybuses that tended to be used on routes with lighter loadings. Despite the 'No Waiting' notice at Bushey Road terminus, No 492 is waiting to take up a route 654 journey to Crystal Palace on 1 October 1955.** *David Clarke*

Below: **No 492 is seen again, this time at the Crystal Palace terminus of route 654 on 10 March 1956. Peek, Frean & Co was established in Bermondsey in 1857 by James Peek and George Hender Frean. The company moved to a larger plant in Bermondsey in 1866, where it continued baking until the brand was discontinued in 1989. In 1861 Peek, Frean introduced the Garibaldi biscuit, and in 1910 introduced its first cream sandwich biscuit, now known as the Bourbon. In 1921 the company entered into an amalgamation agreement with rival biscuit firm Huntley & Palmer, resulting in the creation of a holding company, Associated Biscuit Manufacturers Ltd, although both firms retained their own brands and premises. During the course of its life the firm's brand name changed from Peek, Frean & Co to Peek Frean, then Peek Freans.** *David Clarke*

Top: **This is No 526 (DLY 526), a Class D3 BRCW-bodied Leyland that entered service in August 1937. It is working route 630 to West Croydon on 1 October 1955, a little over seven months before it was withdrawn. I think the parked lorry is a Morris Commercial LC3.** *David Clarke*

Middle: **Also working route 630 to West Croydon on the same day is another D3 Class BRCW-bodied Leyland, No 529 (DLY 529). This trolleybus was in service in August 1937 and was withdrawn during January 1959. The last day of trolleybus operations on the 630 route between Harlesden and West Croydon was 20 July 1960.** *David Clarke*

Bottom: **No 560 (DLY 560), a Class E1 AEC 664T with Brush bodywork, is working service 660 to Hammersmith on 8 August 1956, at The Thatched House pub on Atwood Road. No 560 was new in May 1937 and withdrawn from service in August 1959.** *David Clarke*

Right: **By the time this view was taken in New Barn Street in West Ham on 21 March 1959, the first trolleybus routes to be withdrawn, 654, 696 and 698, had been gone for a little over two weeks. Approaching the camera is No 593 (DLY 593), an E1 Class Brush-bodied AEC 664T that entered service in November 1937 and was withdrawn in February 1960. On the other side of the road is a J1 Class Metro-Cammell-bodied AEC 664T, new in February 1938 and withdrawn in November 1959. Route 687 from Walthamstow to the Victoria & Albert Docks was last operated by trolleybuses on 27 April 1960.** *David Clarke*

Below: **Under a mass of wires at The Bell in Walthamstow on 29 October 1955 is No 643 (DLY 643), a Class E3 AEC 664T with Metro-Cammell bodywork new in May 1937. This** trolleybus was badly damaged in 1944 and rebodied by NCB, and was withdrawn in May 1959. *David Clarke*

Above: This is Brentford High Street on 8 September 1956, and approaching the camera, on a short working of route 655, is No 675 (DLY 675), a Class F1 Metro-Cammell-bodied Leyland LTPB70 that was new in August 1937 and withdrawn and scrapped in May 1959. Working route 657 to Shepherds Bush is No 1889 (LYH 889), a Q1 Class Metro-Cammell-bodied BUT 9641T that entered service in October 1952 and was withdrawn in January 1961, and subsequently sold to Bilbao. *David Clarke*

Below: About to pick up a very healthy number of passengers on Chiswick High Road on the same day is No 675 (DLY 675), a Class F1 Leyland LTPB70 with Metro-Cammell bodywork, which entered service in August 1937 and was withdrawn and scrapped in May 1959. It is working route 655 to Clapham Junction. The last day of trolleybus operations on this route was 9 November 1960. *David Clarke*

Above: This is Shepherds Bush in August 1960 and working route 607 is No 680 (DLY 680), a Class F1 Leyland LTPB70 that was new in August 1937 and withdrawn in November 1960, when this route ceased trolleybus operations. The trolleybus is advertising Vat 69. In 1882 William Sanderson prepared 100 casks of blended whisky and hired a panel of experts to taste them. The batch from the vat numbered 69 was judged to have the best taste, and the famous blend got its name. The whisky was at first bottled in port wine bottles, and is a mixture of about 40 malt and grain whiskies.

Below: Working route 607 in August 1960 is No 703 (DLY 703), a Class F1 Leyland LPTB70 with Metro-Cammell bodywork that was new in August 1937 and withdrawn in November 1960. *Radio Times*, advertised on the corner shop, was first issued on 28 September 1923, carrying details of BBC radio programmes, and at one time had the largest circulation in Europe. Also of note is the Express Dairies milk vending machine.

Above: **Route 607 ran between Uxbridge and Shepherds Bush, passing through Hillingdon, Hayes, Southall, Hanwell, Ealing and Acton. It opened on 15 November 1936 and ceased operation on 8 November 1960. The route journey time was 66 minutes and the service interval between trolleybuses varied between 3 and 6 minutes. Working the route in August 1960 is No 721 (DLY 721), a Class F1 Leyland LPTB70 with Metro-Cammell bodywork, new in September 1937 and withdrawn in November 1960. Just behind is No 1862 (LYH 862), a Q1 Class BUT 9641T working route 657 to Hounslow.**

Below: **This is the High Road in North Finchley at the junction of the North Circular Road in June 1955. Working route 609 to Moorgate is No 955 (ELB 955), a Class J2 BRCW-bodied AEC 664T that entered service in February 1938 and was withdrawn and scrapped in February 1960. The 609 trolleybus route lasted until 8 November 1961.** *David Clarke*

Above: It is 20 May 1957 and working route 611 to Moorgate is No 1038 (EXV 38), a J3 Class AEC 664T with BRCW bodywork. This trolleybus was new in October 1938, and withdrawn and scrapped in April 1960. *David Clarke*

Below: This is the Aldgate terminus of route 653, and about to take up the journey to Tottenham Court Road in August 1960 is No 1045 (EXV 45), an AEC 664T with BRCW bodywork that was new in October 1938 and

withdrawn in July 1960. The originator of the Jacob's brand name was the small biscuit bakery, W. & R. Jacob, founded in 1881 in Bridge Street, Waterford, Ireland, by William Beale Jacob and his brother Robert. It later moved to Bishop Street in Dublin, with a factory in Peter's Row, and also opened a branch in Liverpool in 1916. In the 1920s the two branches separated, the Dublin branch retaining the W. & R. Jacob name while the Liverpool branch was renamed Jacobs Bakery Ltd. Cream Crackers were first manufacture by William Jacob around 1885.

Above: **This is St John Street near The Angel, Islington, on 14 February 1955. Working route 679 is No 1055 (EXV 55). This J3 Class BRCW-bodied AEC 664T entered service in October 1938 and was withdrawn and scrapped in August 1961. The impressive and elegant building in the background is the Northampton Polytechnic. The Northampton Institute, established in 1894, was named after the Marquess of Northampton, who donated the land on which it was built, between Northampton Square and St John Street. The Institute was established to provide for the education and welfare of the local population. In 1967 the Polytechnic, subsequently the Northampton College of Advanced Technology, received its Royal Charter, becoming The City University to reflect the institution's close links with the City of London.** *David Clarke*

Above: **About to go their separate ways in Dalston on 21 March 1959 are Nos 1081 and 1219. No 1081 (EXV 81) is a K1 Class all-Leyland that entered service in November 1938 and was withdrawn and scrapped in July 1960. No 1219 (EXV 219), a K2 Class all-Leyland, was new in February 1939 and was withdrawn and scrapped in July 1961. Both these trolleybus routes ceased on 19 July 1961.** *David Clarke*

Above: **Working route 630 to West Croydon at Shepherds Bush in early July 1960 is No 1119 (EXV 119), a Class K1 all-Leyland new in February 1939 and withdrawn from service only a few days after this view was taken when route 630 ceased trolleybus operations on 19 July 1960 and was replaced by bus route 220. No 703 (DLY 703) is about to embark on a route 607 journey to Uxbridge.**

Below: **Just arrived at the same spot in early August 1960, on route 607, is No 1152 (EXV 152), a Class K1 all-Leyland trolleybus that was new in March 1939 and withdrawn in July 1961.**

Above: **Working route 557 to Liverpool Street Station on 21 March 1957 at The Bakers Arms in Leyton is No 1274 (EXV 274), a Class K1 all-Leyland that was new in June 1939 and withdrawn in April 1961. The Bakers Arms at the time of this photograph was a Taylor Walker Beers pub. Taylor Walker & Co was founded in 1730 in Stepney as Salmon & Hare, later becoming Hare & Hartford. In 1796 John Taylor acquired Hare's share, and the company took the name Taylor Walker in 1816 when Isaac Walker became a partner. The brewery moved to Fore Street, Limehouse, in 1823 and into the Barley Mow Brewery in 1889. Taylor Walker became a public company in 1927, and in 1930 a reverse take-over by the Cannon Brewery, owned by the Iggulden family, which had more than 600 public houses, most in East London, gave the latter a controlling interest. Taylor Walker was taken over by Ind Coope in 1959 and the Barley Mow Brewery was closed in 1960 and demolished in the mid-1960s.** *David Clarke*

Right: **The last day of trolleybus operations on route 677 from West India**

Dock to Smithfield was 15 April 1959. Just 16 days before the abandonment, No 1300 (EXV 300) is captured at the junction of Essex Road and New North Road. A K1 Class all-Leyland trolleybus, it entered service in June 1939 and was withdrawn in September 1961 and scrapped the following month. Behind it is No 1302 (EXV 302), another K1 that entered service in the same month as No 1300 and was withdrawn and scrapped in November 1961. *David Clarke*

Above: **At the junction of Lea Bridge Road and Church Road on 21 March 1959 on a route 655 journey to Leyton is No 1322 (EXV 322), a K2 Class all-Leyland that entered service in March 1939 and was withdrawn from service and scrapped in November 1961.** *David Clarke*

Below: **Working route 581 to Woodford at the junction of Kingsland High Street and Balls**

Pond Road on 21 March 1957 is No 1338 (EXV 338), another K2, which was new in June 1939 and withdrawn in June 1961. The Barclays Bank is still there, a business that can trace its origins back to 1690; the name 'Barclays' became associated it in 1736. Barclays is now ranked as the 21st largest company in the world. *David Clarke*

Above: **This is Mare Street in Hackney on 21 March 1959, and working route 581 is No 1344 (EXV 344), a K2 Class all-Leyland new during June 1939 and withdrawn and scrapped in November 1961.** *David Clarke*

Below: **Working route 517 to Holborn Circus on the High Road, North Finchley, at the crossing of the North Circular Road on 8 August 1956 is No 1370 (EXV 370). This trolleybus is a Class L2 AEC with Metro-Cammell bodywork; it was new in June 1939 and withdrawn in August 1961, just a few months after trolleybus operations ceased on route 517. The trolleybus passing in the opposite direction is No 1266 (EXV 266), a Class K1 all-Leyland that was also new in June 1939, and withdrawn in February 1961.** *David Clarke*

Above: **Passing Leyton Town Hall on 24 August 1957 is No 1383 (FXH 383). It is a Class L3 Metro-Cammell-bodied AEC that entered service in September 1939 and was withdrawn and scrapped in November 1961. The last day of operations of route 699, Chingford Mount to the Docks, was 27 April 1960. The design** competition for Leyton Town Hall attracted **more than 30 architects, and the brief finally went to John Johnson, whose design of red brick and Portland stone was started in 1894. It was opened by the Duke and Duchess of York on 18 March 1896, at a cost of £17,286.** *David Clarke*

Left: **The wartime RTs, RT 2 to RT 151, were AEC Regent IIIs with Chiswick bodywork, and were delivered between October 1939 and February 1942. This batch of buses had a 16ft 4in wheelbase and were fitted with a six-cylinder 9.6-litre diesel engine. This is RT 24 (FXT 199) at Mitcham Common on 1 October 1955. This bus entered service from Putney depot in March 1940 and worked from that depot for a number of years. From the middle of 1950 it became a driver trainer and worked from many depots in this role until 1959, when it was stored at Hounslow. It was finally sold to Birds of Stratford-upon-Avon in September 1960.** *David Clarke*

Above: **Working route 665 to Bloomsbury on 24 August 1957 is No 1469 (FXH 469), negotiating road works in East Street, Barking – note the exposed former tram tracks. No 1469 is an L3 Class Metro-Cammell-bodied AEC that was new in June 1940 and withdrawn in January 1962. The last day of trolleybus operation on route 665 was 11 November 1959.** *David Clarke*

Below: **This is Forest Gate station on the same day, and working route 687 to the Docks is No 1522 (FXH 522), a Class L3 AEC with Metro-Cammell bodywork. It was new in June 1940 and remained in service until the end of trolleybus operations in London in May 1962. Forest Gate station was first opened in 1840 and closed three years later, but after pressure from residents in the area it reopened on 31 May 1846.** *David Clarke*

Right: **Seen at Manor Park Broadway on 24 August 1957, working route 663 to Ilford, is No 1597 (FXH 597). This Class N1 BRCW-bodied AEC 644T was new in November 1939, was withdrawn in January 1962, and scrapped the next month. The parked van is a Ford, and behind is an Austin/Morris LD. This model, which replaced the K8 25cwt Three-way van, was sold under both the Morris and Austin banner and was produced in Birmingham at Adderley Park. The Austin was badged as the 1-ton van (LD1) and the 1.5-ton (LD2), and they were launched in December 1954. Initially the LD was only available with a petrol engine of 2.2 litres, but at the beginning of 1955 both were available with a 2.2-litre diesel engine as an option. The LD2's larger capacity was achieved with a raised roof and a longer body; it also had stiffer suspension all round, and a lower rear axle ratio. The LD continued for another five years until April 1960, when the next major update was the introduction of the four-speed all-synchromesh gearbox. In 1967 the LD range was replaced by the EA model.** *David Clarke*

Below: **This wonderful view of Stratford Broadway was taken on 29 October 1955. Getting a jump start on the cars is No 1616 (FXH 616), a Class N1 BRCW-bodied AEC 644T that was new in November 1939 and withdrawn and scrapped in January 1962. The cars are, I think, a Ford, a Morris and a Jowett. The 40-foot-high granite obelisk in the background, originally with a drinking fountain and a horse trough, was designed by Mr J. Bell and erected in 1861 as a memorial to the late Samuel Gurney by his fellow parishioners.** *David Clarke*

Above: Route 662 ran from Sudbury to Paddington Green through Wembley, Stonebridge Park, Craven Park, Harlesden, Kensal Green, Royal Oak and Harrow Road, and was replaced on 2 January 1962 by bus route 18. Working route 662 in August 1960 is No 1646 (FXH 646), a Class N2 AEC 664T with Park Royal bodywork that was new in November 1939 and was withdrawn at the closure of operations on route 662 in January 1962.

Below: Working route 625 to Wood Green at the Woodford New Road and Forest Road junction on 29 October 1957 is No 1651 (FXH 651). This N2 Class Park Royal-bodied AEC 644T was new in November, withdrawn in January 1962 and scrapped a couple of months later. The car on the left is a Ford Zodiac/Zephyr and the bus is an ECW-bodied Bristol LS. *David Clarke*

Above: **This excellent view shows No 1655 approaching Archway Tavern on route 517 to Holborn. The trolleybus, FXH 655, is an N2 Class Park Royal-bodied AEC 644T, and was new in November 1939; it was withdrawn in January 1962. In the background is the imposing structure of Whittington Hospital; this has its origins in the Small Pox & Vaccination Hospital, built in 1848. Other independently managed hospitals were founded on the Archway and Highgate sites, and in 1946 all were brought together. The hospital was named after Dick Whittington, and its logo incorporates the famous cat.** *David Clarke*

Below: **Working a short route 685 to Silvertown Station is No 1660 (FXH 660), a Class N2 AEC 664T with Park Royal bodywork, which was new in November 1939 and withdrawn in January 1962. The photograph was taken in Church Road, Leyton, on 24 August 1957. Silvertown station was opened on 19 June 1863 by the Eastern Counties & Thames Junction Railway with two tracks. In 1980 this was reduced to one track, and on 9 December 2006 the station closed.** *David Clarke*

Above: This very busy scene, recorded on 1 October 1955, is the West Croydon terminus of route 630 to Harlesden. No 1707 (GGP 707) is a Class P1 Leyland LPTB70 with Metro-Cammell bodywork, new in March 1941 and withdrawn in April 1961. The large car to the left of the trolleybus is a Jaguar Mark IV; built between 1945 and 1949, it was a relaunch of a pre-Second World War model made by SS Cars Ltd from 1936. Before the war the name Jaguar was the model name given to the complete range of cars built by SS Cars Ltd. The saloons were titled SS Jaguar 1½-litre, 2½-litre or 3½-litre, while the two-seater sports car was the SS Jaguar 100 2½-litre or 3½-litre. After the war the company name was changed to Jaguar Cars Ltd. While the post-war saloons were officially the Jaguar 1½-litre, 2½-litre, etc, the term Mark IV was sometimes applied retrospectively by the trade simply to differentiate them from the officially named Mark V. *David Clarke*

Below: This is Romford Road in Ilford on 24 August 1957, and No 1737 is on its way to Barking on route 693. The trolleybus, GLB 737, is a Class SA2 Metro-Cammell-bodied Leyland TT8 that was built for export to South Africa, but was diverted to London service in April 1942. It was withdrawn in August 1959, and was scrapped by January 1960. The large tractor unit in the forecourt to the left is a Scammell. *David Clarke*

Above: **This is No 1758 (GLB 758), a Class SA3 AEC 664T with 8-foot-wide Metro-Cammell bodywork, at the Chadwell Heath terminus of route 693 to Barking on 24 August 1957. The London Co-op was formed in September 1920 by the amalgamation of the Stratford and the Edmonton Co-operative Societies, two of the largest in the London Metropolitan area. By 1952 the London Co-op and its associated Cooperative organisations, the major being the London Co-operative Chemists Limited, had more than 550 establishments of sales and services, varying from large department stores to small grocery shops; they included grocers, butchers, fruit, vegetable and flower sellers, coal depots, furniture sellers, drapers, tailors, footwear sellers, chemists, laundries, estate agencies, funeral services and even guest houses. The London Society also administered many manufacturing and processing establishments. It was amalgamated with the Co-operative Retail Society in 1981.** *David Clarke*

Below: **Between March and October 1946 London Transport took delivery of 50 Weymann-bodied AEC Regals with a 17ft 6in wheelbase and fitted with an AEC 7.7-litre diesel engine and crash gearbox. They were numbered T 719 to T 768 (HGF 809 to HGF 858), and working route 222 at Uxbridge station in July 1955 is T 762, (HGF 852). This bus entered service during September 1946 and was initially allocated to Muswell Hill, but later moved to Uxbridge. It was withdrawn and stored by January 1959 and was bought by the Ceylon Transport Board.** *David Clarke*

Above: **Uxbridge was the last outpost of the Weymann-bodied AEC Regals, where they were the main rolling stock for routes 222, 224, 224A and 224B, including service trips to London Airport. The last were withdrawn as a bunch in November 1958, following the drastic service cuts after that year's strike. All this group of 24 from Uxbridge, together with three trainers from Tottenham, were sold to the Ceylon Transport Board and exported. Seen at Uxbridge station in July 1955 is**

No T 765 (HGF 855); this bus had a claim to fame, as it can be seen on the 1950s film *Genevieve*. *David Clarke*

Below: **Working route 667 from Hammersmith to Hampton Court on 8 August 1956 at Kew Bridge station is No 1792 (HYM 792), a Class Q1 BUT 9641T with Metro-Cammell bodywork; new in April 1948 and withdrawn in April 1961, it was exported to Tarragona in Spain.** *David Clarke*

Main picture: **Route 667 ran from Hampton Court to Hammersmith via Hampton, Fulwell, Twickenham, Isleworth, Brentford, Kew Bridge, Chiswick, Turnham Green, Stamford Brook and Ravenscourt Park. Working this route at Beech Avenue in Brentford on 8 August 1956 is No 1814 (HYM 814), a Class Q1 BUT 9641T with Metro Cammell bodywork; new in July 1948, it was withdrawn in April 1961 and exported to Pontevedra in Spain.**
David Clarke

Below: **The RTWs had the distinction of being London's first 8-foot-wide motor buses. There had been 8-foot-wide buses in London Transport already, but those were trolleybuses, meant for South Africa, which were diverted to London Transport because of the war. They were banned from Central London and spent their days in the Ilford**

area. Similarly, the 8-foot Leylands were originally banned from Central London, and from anywhere with tram tracks, which limited their scope somewhat. They first appeared in May 1949, the first at Tottenham for route 41, which came no further in than Archway. It took until August to stock route 41 completely. Then it was the turn of Alperton, which took two dozen for route 187 in August and September 1949. Shepherds Bush and Hanwell then stocked up for route 105. In October Leyton took 13 for route 144, followed by eight at Enfield in November for route 144A, with West Green taking the next 15 to complete these two routes. December saw them go to Palmers Green for route 112, south of the river for the first time to Putney Bridge for route 85, and to Harrow Weald for routes 140 and 142.

The ban on the use of wide buses in the central zone had arisen because of fears of accidents and congestion in narrow streets. To convince the Public Carriage Office that the fears were groundless, London Transport persuaded it to permit an experiment. Using a single bus would not work, as the fears concerned passing on corners, so eight whole routes passing Notting Hill Gate were swapped from RTs to RTWs for a

week in May 1950. The first experiment was successful enough for two more to follow in June/July. In the second, the area chosen was Shaftesbury Avenue in the West End. Following immediately was a third area, centred on Threadneedle Street in the City for a week. The experiments were a success, and the RTWs were henceforth allowed in the Central zone. However, they were still banned from sharing routes with trams, which cut out much of south-east London, but in the West End and City they were now welcome.

This is RTW 49 (KGK 549), an all-Leyland PD2/3 new in August 1949 and seen here in Victoria Street working route 76 on 28 July 1955. This bus was originally allocated to Alperton, and was used for all three tests. By May 1951 it was transferred to Tottenham to work on routes 34B and 76, and remained

there until 1957, when it was transferred to Upton Park. From late 1963 it became a trainer at a number of depots and survived in this role until it was sold for scrap in December 1969.
David Clarke

Below: **This is Westminster on 28 July 1955, and working route 29 to Victoria Station is RTL 22 (JXN 342), a Park Royal-bodied Leyland PD2/1 new in December 1948. The PD2 chassis was reshaped to fit standard RT bodies, and they were fitted with RT-type air brakes and an AEC transmission. The RTLs ran on route 29 until RTs replaced them on 3 January 1962. This bus was noted in June 1962 working route 170, on which RTLs operated until the end of 1966. The last two RTLs, Nos 543 and 1215, were withdrawn in November 1968.**
David Clarke

Above: **This is RT 1561 (KLB 633), a Park Royal-bodied AEC Regent III, and it is seen in Romford working route 87 to Barking on 13 August 1976. This bus began its service life in November 1949 from Old Kent Road depot, where it stayed until February 1956. Just over 20 years later, and with 12 different depot allocations behind it, it arrived at Barking depot in July 1976, where it remained until withdrawal in September 1978. The last AEC Regent IIIs ran from Barking depot on 7 April 1979. The contrast between the RT and the Daimler Fleetline in the background is, I think, quite startling.**

Right: **This is Victoria Station on 28 July 1955, and working route 25 is RT 1306 (KLB 155), a Saunders roofbox-bodied AEC Regent III new in January 1950. The bus was initially allocated to Forest Gate for route 25 and worked from that depot until overhaul in October 1957. Thereafter it worked from a number of depots including Brixton,** Merton, Croydon and Thornton Heath until it was stored at Kingston in May 1971 and sold for scrap two months later. Working route 52 alongside RT 1306 is RT 3765 (NLE 876), a Weymann-bodied AEC Regent III. *David Clarke*

Below: **RT 1518 (KGK 777), a Craven's roofbox-bodied AEC Regent III, is seen at the West Croydon terminus of route 75 to Woolwich on 1 October 1955. These were rather different buses from the rest of the RTs, the main difference being the five bays between bulkheads. The lower deck windows were not only shorter but deeper, giving a waist-rail lower than on the cab, and the front bulkhead window was substantially shallower. A standard RT cab did not match properly under the Craven's upper deck, which did not taper in at the front like other RTs. This made the upper windows at the front wider, and the back of the bus lacked the upright nature of the RT, curving forwards for the whole of the upper deck; the platform window was appreciably narrower. This bus was new in February 1950 and allocated to Forest Gate; it was transferred to Catford in November 1952, but by June 1956 was stored, then sold to Bird's of Stratford-upon-Avon by August. Shortly afterwards it was purchased by Grey's Coaches of Mildenhall in Suffolk and, after having its roofbox removed and platform doors fitted, entered service in September 1957. The bus was withdrawn and sold for scrap in 1971.** *David Clarke*

Below: **This is RTL 808 (KYY 778), a Metro-Cammell-bodied Leyland PD2/1 new in mid-1950. London Transport had intended to give the entire order of 1,000 RTLs to Metro-Cammell, but that company only completed 450 and Park Royal completed the rest. The Metro-Cammell bodies were almost standard RT bodies and could be recognised by a thicker beading above the cream strip. This view was taken at Trafalgar Square on 28 July 1955, with the bus working route 59A to the Black Horse at Addiscombe.** *David Clarke*

Right: **At Westminster in late July 1955, the bus approaching the camera is RF3 (LUC 203), a Metro-Cammell-bodied AEC Regal IV that was new in May 1951 and initially allocated to Upton Park depot. By June 1953 it had been transferred to Victoria, and in June 1955 was overhauled and painted plain green. The private-hire RFs, besides being the first, were very distinctive. They were only 27ft 6in long, instead of the 30 feet of all the others, and they had glazed cant panels in the sides of the roof. They were needed urgently for the Festival of Britain private hire business starting in May 1951. Some made it in time for the first day, and all 25 had been delivered by 1 June. The new buses certainly looked distinctive, in a livery of Lincoln green below the waist and flake grey above. The curving window surrounds were in flake grey, lined with two thin strips of red. The London Transport fleet name and the bull's-eye motifs on the radiator filler flap and rear door were also in red. Inside, the decor was intended to be light, with green up to waist level, pale green up to just above the windows, and a cream ceiling.**

The buses settled down to work, including operation of the London River Tour, which involved a crossing of the Woolwich Free Ferry. Tours such as this and the West End Seeing London Tour made good use of the glazed roof panels, but London Transport was prohibited by law from using them for excursions beyond the London area, so Windsor, Ascot and Epping Forest were about as far out as they got. This bus was sold to PVS of Ilford in early 1964 and was bought by Premier Travel of Cambridge. By August 1967 it was being used as a source of spares, and was scrapped in early 1970. *David Clarke*

Below: **This is East Croydon station on 23 September 1975, and working route 54 between Woolwich and Selsden is RT 2617 (LYF 342), a Park Royal-bodied AEC Regent III. It was initially allocated to Turnham Green in August 1951, staying there until 1957. A succession of allocations saw the bus at Peckham, New Cross, Loughton, Muswell Hill, Southall and Brixton. During late 1967 the bus received a Weymann body. Further allocations included Willesden, Hendon and Sidcup, and by May 1975 the bus was at Catford depot. It was withdrawn in April 1977 and by August of that year was in Germany.**

Right: **Working route 36 at Victoria on 28 July 1955 is RT 2845 (LYF 492), at this time a Park Royal-bodied AEC Regent III, which was initially allocated to Rye Lane depot in April 1952. Route 36 ran between West Kilburn and Hither Green station and was operated by RTs until mid-February 1963. During 1957 RT 2845 was transferred to Hendon, then to Potters Bar and Catford. It received a Weymann body during overhaul in mid-1968 and worked from Sidcup and Bromley depots until it was stored in June 1973 and sold for scrap two months later. I think the car behind is a 1951 Buick. It was in 1813 in Leith, Edinburgh, that William Crawford founded Crawford biscuits.** *David Clarke*

Below: **This is Chiswick High Road at the junction of Chiswick Lane on 8 August 1956, and working route 657 to Hounslow is No 1869 (LYH 869), a Class Q1 BUT 9641T with Metro-Cammell bodywork new in October 1952, withdrawn in January 1961 and exported to Bilbao in Spain. The partially visible car on the** left is, I think, a Standard Eight, which when launched in 1953 cost £481 including taxes. The car travelling in the opposite direction is a Vauxhall E; in 1956 you could purchase one for £931 including taxes. Did you know that 'kia ora' is a Maori greeting meaning 'be well/healthy', and is used for both 'hello' and 'goodbye'? The drink was first created in Australia in 1903 and was launched in the UK in 1917. *David Clarke*

Right: **Route 657 was one of the eight trolleybus routes that ran for the last time on 8 May 1962. This is Chiswick High Road on 8 September 1956, and working 657 is No 1871 (LYH 871), a Q1 Class Metro-Cammell-bodied BUT 9641T, new in October 1952. After less than nine years in service it was sold to Bilbao during January 1961.** *David Clarke*

Below: **Also working route 657 to Hounslow on 8 August 1956, at the junction of Goldhawk Road and Hammersmith Grove, is No 1872 (LYH 872), a Class Q1 BUT 9641T with Metro-Cammell bodywork. New in November 1952, it was withdrawn in February 1961 and exported to San Sebastian in Spain. Note the Firestone logo on the bridge in the background, a common site in the 1950s. The company was originally based in Akron, Ohio, which was also the home town of its arch-rival, Goodyear. The company began operations in 1900 with 12 employees, and in 1906 Firestone tyres were chosen by Henry Ford for the Model T. Together, Firestone and Goodyear were the largest suppliers of automotive tyres in North America for more than three-quarters of a century. At one point, the company had a rubber plantation in Liberia that covered more than 4,000sq km. In 1928 the company built a factory in Brentford, but this closed in 1979, and in 1988 the company was sold to the Japanese Bridgestone Corporation.** *David Clarke*

Above: This is Chiswick Roundabout on the same day, and working route 657 to Shepherds Bush is No 1883 (LYH 883), another Q1 that was new in December 1952, withdrawn in January 1961, and subsequently sold to Bilbao in Spain. Note the National Provincial Bank in the background, which first operated in 1833, and the first branch to open was in Gloucester on 1 January 1834. By the turn of the century the bank had 250 offices in England and Wales. Considered one of the big five, it expanded during the 19th and 20th centuries and took over a number of smaller banking companies. The National Provincial was merged with the Westminster Bank and named the National Westminster; NatWest, as it became known, is now part of the Royal Bank of Scotland Group. *David Clarke*

Below: This Q1 BUT 9641T with Metro-Cammell bodywork is No 1890 (LYH 890), new in December 1952 and seen in Chiswick High Road in August 1956. Numerically the second-last London trolleybus, No 1890 was withdrawn in February 1961 and exported to San Sebastian. A total of 125 Q1 trolleybuses were exported to Spain, of which 112 entered service. *David Clarke*

Above: **Also on 8 August 1956, No 1889 (LYH 889) is seen working on route 657 at Goldhawk Road. A Q1 Class Metro-Cammell-bodied BUT 9641T, it entered service in December 1952 and was withdrawn in February 1961, being sold to Bilbao. In total, there were 1,891 trolleybuses in the London Transport fleet, comprising 41 classes, seven experimental vehicles, and 13 different bodybuilders. At the peak of trolleybus operations there were 22 depots providing 74 daytime routes (including seven night routes), totalling 235 miles.** *David Clarke*

Below right: **A total of 76 Weymann low-height AEC Regent IIIs were delivered to London Transport between May 1950 and December 1952. The first batch of 20, RLH 1 to 20 (KYY 501 to 520), had roof ventilators and added trafficators. They also originally had the front numberplates mounted below the chromed radiators, roll-up radiator blinds, and no rear-wheel discs. The route stencil holder on the rear window fell out of use early on. All this class were originally with London Country, but three were later repainted red. The second batch, RLH 21 to 76 (MXX 221 to 276), had polished aluminium radiators rather than chrome. They lacked** the prominent roof-mounted ventilators, but had LT-style used-ticket boxes on the platform. They also had LT double-arrow indicators above the rear numberplate. RLH 21 to 52 were originally green, but five later became red, RLH 53 to 76 were red. This is Upminster in August 1969, and RLH 68 (MXX 268) is working route 248 between Upminster and Cranham. This bus entered service from Merton on route 127 in December 1952 and stayed there until August 1958. Between then and May 1959 it worked from Harrow Weald depot on route 230, then until March 1966 it worked out of the Dalston depot on route 178. The bus returned to Harrow Weald depot from March 1966 until June 1969, then until September 1970 it worked out of Hornchurch depot until routes 248 and 248A were changed

to one-person operation with SMS-type single-deckers. RLH 68 was exported to the USA in June 1971.

Right: Only five RLHs were required for the Upminster 248 and 248A routes. Waiting to take up service in August 1969 on the 248A to Corbets Tey is RLH 71 (MXX 271). This bus was initially allocated to Merton from December 1952 for route 127, and stayed there until August 1958. From then until March 1966 it worked from Harrow Weald on routes 230 and 230A. It transferred to Hornchurch depot in March 1966 to work on routes 248 and 248A, which were converted to SMS one-person operation on 19 September 1970. That then left just one RLH-operated service, route 178 between Clapton Pond and Stratford, with the buses allocated to Dalston. This service ran for the last time in April 1971. RLH 71 was exported to the USA in January 1972. Typhoo tea was launched by John Sumner Junior of Birmingham in 1903, and the brand, now owned by the Apeejay Surrendra Group, is produced at Moreton in the Wirral. Did you know that Typhoo comes from the Chinese word for doctor?

Below: There are not too many traffic lights in sight in Parliament Square in this view taken in late July 1955. The bus working route 88 to Oxford Circus only is RT 3013 (NLE 903), a Park Royal-bodied AEC Regent III that entered service from Middle Row depot in May 1953. It subsequently passed through a number of depots, including Alperton, Hornchurch and finally Holloway, where it was withdrawn in May 1971; it had been sold for scrap by August 1971. *David Clarke*

Right: **This is RT 3766 (NLE 873), a Weymann-bodied AEC Regent III in July 1955 about to turn into Junction Road at the Archway Tavern in Highgate, working route 137 to Clapham Common. From January 1950 until November 1964 this route was operated by RTs and RTLs.** *David Clarke*

Below: **Through the 1970s the number of RTs in service dwindled, but there were still odd occasions when routes were converted to RT operation, such as Enfield on route 217B. As late as January 1976 Seven Kings depot still had a full allocation of RTs. In early 1978 many of the remaining RTs were withdrawn, leaving Harrow Weald, Bromley and Barking as the last depots using them in service. Route 140 was one of the remaining RT routes in 1978, but RT operation finished on it on 15 July. Bromley's RT operations on route 94 finished on 27 August 1978, which** left routes 62 and 87 at Barking as the last bastions of RT passenger operation, finally ceasing on 7 April 1979. Working route 140 between Mill Hill and London Airport Central in September 1962 is RT 4451 (OLD 672), a Park Royal-bodied AEC Regent III. At that time the Heathrow Airport bus terminus was quite basic.

Above: Sitting at Feltham station about to take up a route 237 journey to Sunbury Village on 18 April 1975 is RF 603 (NLE 603). This AEC Regal was new to the Country area during July 1953 and was allocated to Dorking depot. It was converted to one-person operation in October 1957. On 1 January 1969 12 Country RFs were transferred to Muswell Hill to work on route 210, and one of these was RF 603. It was repainted red in June 1969 and remained at Muswell Hill until September 1971. Transferred to Palmers Green, it worked on route 212, then by January 1973 it was at Fulwell, but three months later it was allocated to Hounslow for route 237. When that route was converted to Bristol operation in April 1977, RF 603 was withdrawn by August 1977.

Below left: After the end of the war, London Transport obtained the contract to operate services between Central London and the airports at Heathrow, Croydon and Northolt. The initial fleet comprised Commer Commandos, but these only had seating for 18. In the early 1950s BEA was persuaded by London Transport to purchase a new fleet of coaches. These were AEC Regals with Park Royal 1½-deck bodies and a livery of dark grey and dove grey with a white band between them. A batch of 50 was ordered, and the first entered service in May 1952. A further 15 (NLP 636 to NLP 650), identical to the first batch, arrived between August and October 1953. These coaches shuttled between Waterloo Station and the airports, increasingly to Heathrow, and were maintained at Victoria depot. In 1957 the London terminal changed to Cromwell Road, and the coaches were transferred to Shepherds Bush depot. During 1957-58, when the coaches received an overhaul, the livery was changed to grey and white. In 1960 the fleet was reallocated to the trolleybus depot at Hammersmith, and in July 1966 the coaches were transferred to the old tram depot at Chiswick. This is Heathrow in July 1962, and the nearest in a line-up of BEA coaches is NLP 645. It entered service in October 1953, was withdrawn in March 1967, and was sold to Birds of Stratford-upon-Avon in September of that year. It was then sold to Yardleys, the perfumers, as a staff bus in January 1968, remaining there until April 1977, when it was purchased for preservation.

Right: **This is a rare view of RM 1 (SLT 56), the first AEC Routemaster, working route 2, Golders Green to Crystal Palace, on 11 February 1956, just three days into its service life. The first appearance of the Routemaster prototype was at the Commercial Motor Show in September 1954. It then joined RM 2 on a test programme involving hill starts and 7,500 miles of test running, then made a brief appearance at the Aluminium Industry Exhibition on the South Bank in June 1955. It was licensed as SLT 56 on 11 January 1956, and after a spell of crew training at Cricklewood was allocated to route 2, entering service on 8 February 1956. It continued in service until August, when on the 8th it returned to Chiswick for front-end modification. When it reappeared in public at the Lord Mayor's Show in 1956 it had a vertically mounted radiator behind a vertically slotted grill. The RT engine in RM 1 was also replaced by a new AEC AV600 9.6-litre diesel engine. On 6 March 1957 RM 1 returned to Cricklewood and was used on routes 260 and 2 on Sundays. It was overhauled on 31 July 1959 and returned to training duties only, firstly at Upton Park. Repainted in 1964, it was withdrawn from trainer use at Dalston in 1972. It was sold to the Lockheed Corporation in 1973, but was bought back by London Transport in 1983 for preservation.** *David Clarke*

Right: **It is unusual to see a hand-written route number on a destination display, but RM 591 (WLT 591), a Park Royal-bodied AEC Routemaster, has this oddity in Romford working route 175 to Dagenham on 13 August 1976. New in February 1961, the bus was initially allocated to Highgate depot; it lasted until its withdrawal in July 1986, and was sold for scrap two months later.**

Right: **Working route 174 to Dagenham on 13 August 1976 in Romford is RM 1567 (567 CLT), a Park Royal-bodied AEC Routemaster, which when new in April 1963 had a Leyland O.600 engine. The bus was initially allocated to Rye Lane depot, but by the time of its withdrawal in August 1984 was at Tottenham depot. Three months later it was scrapped.**

Below: **The idea of a front-entrance, rear-engined Routemaster originated in 1964, with a collaboration between London Transport, AEC and Park Royal to develop the bus. The AEC AV691 engine was similar to that developed for the AEC Merlins, and the running gear used components from standard Routemasters rearranged to suit the rear engine with air suspension at the rear. After nearly two years in build, FRM 1 (KGY 4D) made its first public appearance at Christmas 1966. In June 1967 it entered service from Tottenham depot, working on routes 34B and 76. It was well received, but on 31 August 1967 it caught fire and was badly damaged. After repair it returned to Tottenham, remaining there until August 1969. In December it was allocated to Croydon to work the quiet route 233 between West Croydon and Roundshaw, and in March** 1971 it was working route 234. A new route was then found for FRM 1, the local Potters Bar route 284, and it was a popular bus at that depot. This photograph was taken at Potters Bar station on 13 August 1976. The allocation to Potters Bar ceased the following month, when FRM 1 was in collision with London Country's SNB 92, and was taken away for repair. In December 1977 it was fitted with a public address system ready to take up duties on the Round London Sightseeing Tour, which it started early in 1978. FRM 1 was withdrawn from the tour in February 1983 and handed over to the London Museum of Transport the following month.

Right: **Between October and November 1966 British Overseas Airways Corporation (BOAC) took delivery of 15 Metro-Cammell coach-bodied Leyland PDR1/1s (LYF 304D to LYF 318D) for its service between central London and Heathrow. They were originally fitted with 34 coach seats, and seen on 18 April 1975 at Heathrow is LYF 309D. On 31 March 1974 BOAC and British European Airways (BEA) merged to form British Airways, and LYF 309D is seen in BA livery.**

Below: **BEA had for some time operated a service between its London book-in terminal and Heathrow airport, for its domestic and European passengers. It had started the service in the 1950s with Commer Commandos, and continued it with its fleet of RFs. BEA also conducted trials with double-deckers, one an AEC Regent V with a large rear luggage compartment, and the other RMF 1254, with a trailer. BEA now ordered a fleet of 65, together with 88 trailers by Marshall. They were of the standard Routemaster length of 27ft 8in, but were geared for 70mph motorway operation. The driver's front window was a single pane, they had no destination displays, had illuminated panels, and were equipped with paraffin heaters. They entered service** between October 1966 and April 1967 and were based at the Chiswick tram depot. London Transport purchased 13 in August 1975, followed by 14 in September 1976 and a further nine in the summer of 1978. The remainder moved garage to Stonebridge in August 1978, and in March 1979 they were all withdrawn and purchased by London Transport. This view of RMA 9 (NMY 646E) was taken in Romford on 13 August 1976, working route 175 between Dagenham and North Romford. This bus was purchased by London Transport in August 1975 and, after modifications such as removal of the towing gear and luggage racks, entered service from North Street, Romford, depot in October 1975. It was withdrawn from passenger service a month after this view and became a staff bus until its sale to Wembley Stadium in March 1988. It was last noted with Timebus Travel of St Albans in March 2009.

Above: On 18 April 1966 London Transport began Red Arrow limited-stop, high-frequency services between Victoria and Marble Arch, using six Strachan-bodied AEC Merlins; the route number was 500. By 1972 there were eight Red Arrow routes, and one was the 503 between Waterloo Station and Victoria Station. Working this route is MBA 533 (VLW 533G), an MCW-bodied AEC Merlin that entered service from the Merton depot in June 1969. It was transferred via Enfield to Walthamstow by September 1969, and a few months later was converted for the Red Arrow service, and was allocated to Victoria by January 1970. This view is at Terminus Place, Victoria, in May 1972, and the bus remained at Victoria depot until its withdrawal in January 1982. Two months later it was sold to Euro Trac of Wembley, and later became a static cafe near Halifax, but was noted as having been scrapped in 1990.

Right: In their first job the Merlins were an undoubted success. The Red Arrow routes were people-shifters, moving in bulk along good city highways between bus stations with limited stops. This was the job for which the new buses were designed, and they did it well. This is MBA 571, originally registered as VLW 571G in May 1969, but after being stored until August 1969 it was re-registered AML 571H. It was converted for the Red Arrow service and allocated to Victoria depot in January 1970. In this view, taken at Victoria in May 1972, the bus is working route 506 between Victoria Station and Piccadilly Circus. MBA 571 was stored in February 1976 and sold for scrap by July 1977 after a very short service history. From April 1981 Leyland Nationals started to replace the Merlins on the Red Arrow services.

Above: The Merlins were thought to be too long, so London Transport decided to adopt the shorter version of the AEC Swift chassis, giving an overall length of 33ft 5in instead of 36 feet, and an 8.2-litre engine was fitted. In service, the bus proved under-powered, unreliable and expensive to overhaul. The first 50, SM 1 to 50, bodied by Marshall with single doors for suburban RT replacement, entered service from 24 January 1970 from Catford depot. The second batch, SMS 51 to 100, were bodied by Park Royal and had dual doorways; the first entered service from New Cross depot on 18 April 1970. Working route 91 in May 1973 is SMS 171 (EGN 171J), a Marshall dual-doorway AEC Swift that entered service from Enfield depot in October 1970 on route 107. It worked from a number of depots and ended its service life at Hornchurch, where it was withdrawn in July 1977 and was sold for scrap in June 1978 after a very short service life.

Above right: The choice of British chassis for rear-engine buses was Leyland Atlantean or Daimler Fleetline. London Transport had trialled both extensively, in the large XA and small XF classes, since 1965. LT ordered an updated version of the Fleetline, with a modern angular Park Royal body, known as the DMS. London Transport ordered its first

batch of 17 in 1968, but there was a queue. The original batch was fitted with the well-respected transversely mounted Gardner 6LXB engine, and the livery was unrelieved red, in order to allow maximum advertising space. DMS 1 and DMS 2 appeared at the Earl's Court Commercial Motor Show in September 1970, and by December up to DMS 74 had been delivered. The DMS first entered service in January 1970 on routes 95 and 220, with Brixton and Shepherds Bush depots receiving allocations of DMSs. Working route 175 in Romford on 13 August 1976 is DMS 482 (MLK 482L), a Park Royal-bodied Daimler CRG 6LXB, new in November 1972 and allocated to North Street, Romford, depot. The bus remained there for all of its service life, which was terminated in September 1979. In October it was sold to Ensign Bus, and by March 1980 it had been sold to China Motor Bus of Hong Kong.

Right: **By 1972 London Transport had another 1,600 DMSs ordered for delivery over the next three years. Park Royal and Metro-Cammell-Weymann (MCW) shared the body orders, with Park Royal eventually bodying DMS 368 to 1217, and MCW DMS 1218 to 1967. The MCW bodies looked very similar at first glance, but the most apparent difference was the bodywork beadings, especially around the edge of the roof – the MCW had a prominent moulding, while the Park Royals did not. The emergency doors were differently shaped, MCW's being taller with a rounded top, while Park Royal's was square-topped.**

Working route C1 to New Addington at East Croydon station on 23 September 1975 is DMS 1387 (MLH 387L), which had an MCW body and a Leyland O.680 engine. This bus entered service in January 1973 from Croydon depot and remained there until its withdrawal in November 1979, when it was sold for scrap.

Below: **Seen at the same place on the same day, working route 130B to New Addington, DM 1043 (GHV 43N) has bodywork by Park Royal and was originally fitted with a Leyland O.680 engine. It entered service from Croydon depot in March 1975 and spent most of its service life working from there until withdrawal in August 1981. It was sold to** Ensign Bus & Coach some time in 1985 and worked with that company until July 1990, when it was sold again to Frontrunner South East in Dagenham. By March 1992 DM 1043 was with Hadleigh & Spence, Castle Point Buses. Squeezing past the bus is a Renault 4, also known as the 4L. This economy car was produced between 1961 and 1994, and was the first front-wheel-drive family car produced by Renault. By 1 February 1966 1 million cars had been produced. It remained a basic car throughout its life, but did offer a comfortable ride due to well-designed suspension, and had comfortable seats, a powerful heater and effective ventilation.

Right: **In March 1976 the updated design entered service, which had two-piece glider doors in place of the four-piece folding doors, pantograph windscreen wipers on the nearside windscreen, fitted internal fire extinguishers, fluorescent tubes in the blind boxes and a cover over the rear-blind handle. They were also now officially Leyland Fleetlines, rather than Daimler Fleetlines, with emblems to match. They were easy to recognise, as they wore the livery that had been experimentally tried on DMS 46 in 1974, a white surround to the upper-deck windows. DMS 2081 (KJD 81P), which had Park Royal bodywork and a Leyland O.680 engine, is seen in Romford on 13 August**

1976 working route 103 to Rainham. This bus entered service in May 1976 from North Street, Romford, depot and remained allocated to that depot until December 1979, when it was transferred to Seven Kings depot. A few months later it was allocated to Elmers End; it was withdrawn from service in December 1982 and scrapped five months later.

Below: **London Transport still had a number of RF-operated routes that were unsuitable for Leyland Nationals due to width restrictions. The remaining RFs were getting old, passing their quarter-century of intensive town service. The Bristol LH was chosen as a replacement, probably because it was the only narrow bus in production. The BLs were 30-foot-long, 7ft 6in-wide Bristol LH6Ls with Leyland engines and**

automatic gearboxes. They had ECW bodies, with a modified doorway and a destination indicator on the nearside above and behind the doorway. The livery at first was red with white window surrounds and waistband. North Street garage (NS) was the first to get the Bristols, in April 1976, for routes 247 and 250, replacing RTs and RFs respectively. This is BL 12 (KJD 412P) in Romford working route 247 on 13 August 1976. This bus was allocated to North Street, Romford, depot until January 1980 when it was transferred, after overhaul and a repaint to plain red, to Croydon, where it was withdrawn by June 1982. Grampian purchased it in December 1982, then sold it on to Mair in January 1988. Mair sold it in September 1993 to Henley's of Abertillery. Unfortunately, it was fire-damaged by vandals in November 1996 and scrapped.

Right: **This is BL 13 (KJD 413P) in Abridge working route 250 to Epping on the same day. In January 1977 route 250 was withdrawn and amalgamated with route 247. Two BLs were released by this change and one was retained for a new route between Romford Station and Ongar. Both the 247 and the 247B were converted to Leyland National operation in January 1980. At this time BL 13 was overhauled and repainted red, and was allocated to Uxbridge, then Kingston, mostly for training duties. Withdrawn by September 1982, it was sold to Avon Commercial Diesels, and soon afterwards Tally Ho! of Kingsbridge in Devon purchased it. It remained in service with Tally Ho! until 2007 when it was purchased for preservation.**

North Downs Rural Transport

North Downs Rural Transport was a successor to Brown Motor Services, provided by Tom Brady of Forest Green, who had started the business in the 1920s. North Downs acquired Brown Services in 1970 and was based in Orpington, filling in the gaps in services that Southdown, London Transport, London Country and Aldershot & District found unviable.

Right: **North Downs also operated to and around the Horsham area, and former Western Welsh Weymann-bodied Albion Nimbus WKG 48, fleet No 19, is seen in September 1971 at the town centre Carfax terminus in Horsham prior to returning to Forest Green on route 852. This location is now part of a pedestrianised area. Between 1960 and 1961 Western Welsh took delivery of 48 of this type of bus, TUH 1 to 24 bodied by Harrington and WKG 25 to 48 by Weymann. The two batches were almost identical in appearance and seated 30 passengers in high-backed dual-purpose seats; they were spread over the complete Western Welsh network with small numbers allocated to almost every depot, Brecon and Bridgend gaining the largest allocations. The Nimbus had a short life with Western Welsh, and by 1968 around half had been withdrawn.**

Left: **Also in Horsham in September 1971 is MOD 954, an ex-Western National Bristol LS with ECW bodywork, operating the more local service 851 to Rusper. This bus is in brown livery, but with the name 'Tillingbourne Valley' painted at the top of the destination box and a notice in the windscreen explaining that it is on hire to North Downs Rural Transport. Subsequently Tillingbourne Valley took over the routes. This bus entered service with Western National in January 1953 with seating for 35. By October 1953 the seating had been changed to 41, with 19 standing. In April 1965 the bus was converted for one-person operation, and remained so until withdrawal in 1971. It was acquired by Tillingbourne Bus Co Ltd in July and passed to North Downs in December, remaining in service until September 1972, when it passed back to Tillingbourne.**

Orpington & District

Filling a gap where apparently London Transport saw no justification for introducing its own service, North Downs Rural Transport started a route between Orpington and Croydon via Addington in 1969, giving it the route number 853. This continued a sequence of route numbers used by North Downs for a small network of quite separate routes in the Horsham area. A separate service was started the next year linking Croydon with Forestdale, a new housing development just south of Addington and close to the border with Surrey, but this route was taken over by Orpington & District shortly afterwards. Within a few years North Downs was experiencing financial difficulties and sought a merger with Orpington & District, which subsequently took full control of these routes.

Orpington & District fell into financial difficulties, and its services passed to Tillingbourne from February 1981. More experienced management turned the services into a resounding success, and these lucrative operations were separated off into a new company, Metrobus, from 24 September 1983.

Orpington & District introduced full-size buses, and MKG 479, a Willowbrook-bodied Leyland PSUC1/2 new to Western Welsh in 1956, is seen on 23 September 1975 at Croydon on the Forestdale route. This bus was part of a batch of ten PSUC1/2s, originally numbered 472 to 483, which were delivered with dual-purpose seating.

Above: The 'lowbridge' Leyland PDR1/1 was introduced in 1961 and continued until the PDR1/2 was introduced in 1964. This new chassis did away with the sunken gangway at the rear of the upper deck while maintaining the overall height of 13ft 6in. A total of 344 'lowbridge' PDR1/1s were built on the Leyland PDR1/1 chassis, and the largest operator was Potteries, which purchased 105. East Midland took delivery of 32, Nos 130 to 161 (130 to 139 BRR and 140 to 149 ENN, and between January and February 1961 150 to 161 HRR). Orpington & District used double-deckers and 157 HRR, a Weymann-bodied Leyland Atlantean purchased from East Midland in 1977, is seen at Bardolph Avenue, Forestdale, in April 1978.

Below: Forestdale was served at certain times of day by route No 857, a deviation of the through Croydon to Orpington journeys. Picking up a very healthy number of passengers in Croydon on 7 January 1978 is Park Royal dual-purpose-bodied AEC Reliance 417 DHO. This bus had been new to Aldershot & District in March 1962 and later passed to the South Midland fleet of City of Oxford, from whom Orpington & District purchased it in 1974.

Rover Bus Sevice

Mr J. R. G. Dell founded Rover Bus in 1928 following a period of service with the London General Omnibus Company. This well-known independent operator in the Hemel Hempstead area ran the service between Hemel Hempstead bus station and Chesham Broadway. The direct route from Chesham to Hemel Hempstead via Whelpley Hill was jointly operated with London Transport until 6 May 1964 (a very rare instance of a joint LT working), while the service via Boxmoor, Bovingdon, Flaunden, Latimer and Lye Green had always been a Rover operation. By February 1969 Rover was providing a daily service, generally hourly (2-hourly on Sundays), although not all journeys served Flaunden and Latimer. During 1986 the services became Hertfordshire County Council routes 51 and 52.

Below: **Passing Bovingdon Primary School in July 1972 is LBL 701, which is, I think, a Bedford SBG with Duple Midland bodywork. The SB was launched at the 1950 Commercial Motor Show as the replacement for the OB, and was the first Bedford PSV chassis to be offered with a choice of petrol and diesel engines. The standard petrol engine was the Bedford six-cylinder 4.927, which was to remain in production throughout the life of the SB. Several variants of diesel engines could be fitted to the SB, all with six cylinders. The SB in all its variations was produced for 37 years until the close of Bedford production in 1987.**

Above: In the same month in the same village, VBH 666J, a Plaxton-bodied Ford R192 purchased new by Rover in January 1971, is turning from Green Lane into Bovingdon High Street.

Below: Rover Bus Service purchased WBM 744K, a Willowbrook-bodied Ford R192, new in May 1972, and it is seen leaving the High Street in Bovingdon and entering Green Lane en route to Chesham, with a reasonable number of passengers, also in July 1972.

Southdown Motor Services

Southdown Motor Services Ltd was formed in 1915 as the result of a merger between the Brighton, Hove & Preston United Omnibus Co, Sussex Tourist Coaches (which had been renamed in 1913 from Worthing Motor Services of 1909, itself successor to the Sussex Motor Road Car Co of 1904), and the London & South Coast Haulage Co Ltd, which had been founded in 1912. Expansion was quick and by 1924 regular express services began between Brighton and London. It was a Southdown coach that was the first vehicle to enter Victoria Coach Station on 10 March 1932.

In 1929 the company started a coastal express service between Bournemouth and Margate jointly with East Kent Road Car and Hants & Dorset. This service was later to become known as the South Coast Express and continued until NBC days. Southdown gained services previously operated by East Surrey in East Grinstead and Crawley, and this also extended the company's eastern boundary to Heathfield. Southdown became associated with BET following the division of Tilling and BET in 1942. In 1946 a coordination agreement with Portsmouth Corporation was reached, splitting mileage and receipts on a 57% to 43% share, Southdown being the minority.

This replaced an earlier agreement dating from 1931 involving protective fares on Southdown routes within the city. The coordination of services, dubbed Portsmouth Area Joint Transport Services, lasted until deregulation in 1986.

In 1950 Southdown operated its first overseas tour to France and Switzerland, and that year also saw the introduction of scenic open-top services from Brighton to Devil's Dyke and from Eastbourne to Beachy Head. In 1957 Southdown also entered into the Heathfield Pool agreement with Maidstone & District, whereby all services through Heathfield became joint operations. In 1958 mileage agreements were reached with London Transport for services in Crawley, and with Brighton, Hove & District and Brighton Corporation for services that established the Brighton Area Transport Services.

It was during the late 1950s and 1960s that Southdown purchased many of the vehicle types most commonly associated with the company, notably the Leyland PD3 'Queen Mary' vehicles. In 1964 Southdown moved into new headquarters in Freshfield Road, which also became the headquarters of Brighton, Hove & District in 1969 when that company passed to Southdown.

Opposite top: **This busy view of Upperton Road in Eastbourne was taken in July 1961. Nearest the camera is No 55 (DHC 655), an East Lancashire-bodied AEC Regent V new to Eastbourne Corporation in the early spring of 1956. It was one of a batch of seven, the first 8-foot-wide buses purchased by Eastbourne. The Southdown bus on the right, LUF 737, is an all-Leyland PD2 new to Southdown in the very early 1950s. Just behind is No 1514**

(MCD 514), an East Lancashire-bodied Leyland PSU1/13, which was new to Southdown in 1953 as a dual-purpose centre-entrance bus, and was subsequently rebuilt as a one-person-operated bus with a front entrance in 1959.

Opposite bottom: **Towards the end of 1953 Southdown took delivery of a batch of Northern Counties-bodied Leyland PD2/12s, and representing this batch is No 757 (MUF**

457). This excellent view, showing the bus working the quite long stage service 22 to Midhurst, was taken in the summer of 1966. The car following No 757 is an Austin A35, which was introduced in 1956 as a replacement for the Austin A30. It was very similar in appearance, except for a larger rear window aperture and a painted front grille, with a chrome horseshoe surround instead of the chrome grille featured on the A30. The semaphore signal indicators were later replaced with front-and-rear-mounted flashing lights.

Right: **Working route 38 to Bevendean Hospital in the spring of 1967 is No 766 (OCD 766), a Park Royal-bodied Leyland PD2/12 that was new to Southdown in May 1955. Bevendean Hospital originally opened in 1881 as a smallpox sanatorium, and the main buildings followed in 1898. The institution continued as the Brighton Borough Hospital until take over by the NHS in 1948. It closed to inpatients in April 1989, and the buildings, which still stand in Bear Road and Bevendean Road, are scheduled for redevelopment as housing. The car on the right is a Morris Minor, and the car partially visible on the left of No 766 is an Triumph 2000 Mark I, which was presented to the public at the London Motor Show in October 1963 with production starting in January 1964 and ending in 1969 when just over 120,000 had been produced.**

Below: **Pool Valley, Brighton, was such a small area for buses, and always a busy area, with buses reversing all over the place. I seem to remember from my days in Brighton the plastic canopy over the waiting area, and the mannequin dressed as a conductor at the** entrance to the toilets. Seen when new in the early winter of 1960, nearest the camera is Brighton, Hove & District No 10, which was one of three Bristol FS6Bs, Nos 9 to 11 (RPN 9 to 11) that were convertible open-toppers. Next in line is Southdown No 520 (OUF 520), a Guy Arab IV with Park Royal bodywork, very pleasing to the eye and new in 1955. The bus going to take up the long journey to Gravesend is Maidstone & District DH 387 (NKT 883), an all-Leyland PD2/12 new in 1951.

Right: **The date is 7 August 1956 and approaching the camera, near Newick, is No 523 (OUF 523), a Park Royal-bodied Guy Arab IV new to Southdown in 1955. These buses went into production in 1951, and a large number had concealed radiators, but Southdown retained the exposed radiator.**

Right: **In late 1956 Southdown took delivery of 12 Beadle-bodied Leyland PD2/12s, Nos 777 to 788 (RUF 177 to 188). They were built on Park Royal frames, and I think I am correct in saying that they were the last double-deckers to be built by Beadle, and probably the last ever examples of Beadle bus bodywork completed. The lorry in the background is a Bedford TJ, which was first manufactured in 1958, and was still available until 1975.**

Below: **During 1957 Southdown took delivery of 40 Beadle-bodied Leyland PSUC1/2s with O.350 5.76-litre engines. They were numbered 1075 to 1114 (SUF 875 to 914), and seen heading for Bournemouth in the summer of 1967 is No 1102 (SUF 902). It was originally allocated to the Triumph Coaches fleet and was numbered T1102. It was returned to Southdown livery in 1966, and withdrawn and sold to Wimpey in 1968. The three-wheeler on the other side of the road is a Reliant Regal 3/25, which had been introduced in October** 1962; unlike previous Regals it no longer had a wooden frame, but instead had a unitary construction body of reinforced fibreglass, which was moulded in two major units (outer and inner), then bonded together and bolted to a steel chassis.

Right: **During 1956 and 1957 Southdown took delivery of 25 Beadle 'Rochester'-bodied Commer coaches with TS 3 three-cylinder opposed-piston two-stroke diesel engines. The first five, Nos 1 to 5 (RUF 101 to 105), had centre-entrance doorways, while Nos 6 to 25 (TCD 6 to 15 and TUF 16 to 25) had front entrances. This is No 15 (TCD 15), which was withdrawn in 1969 and sold to Thyssen of Llanelli in that year.**

The John C. Beadle company was founded in 1894 in Dartford and produced horse-drawn vehicles. By 1930 it employed between 300 and 400 people and produced bodies for commercials, private and passenger vehicles, but ceased trading in 1957. The development of the Commer TS3 engine was by Eric W. Coy, Rootes' chief engineer at the Humber plant at Stoke Aldermoor, Coventry. The 'TS' stands for Tilling Stevens, which was acquired by Rootes in 1950; from 1954 Rootes diesel engine manufacture was moved to the Tilling Stevens factory in Maidstone. The TS 3 was a two-stroke diesel engine that produced 105bhp and gained a reputation for good performance.

Below: **This view of Beadle-bodied Commer No 21 (TUF 21) was taken in the summer of 1967. In 1969 this bus was sold by Southdown to I.**

C. Margo of Penge, and was later noted with Nu-Venture coaches in Maidstone in 1971. The invalid carriage on the left is a Tippen Delta produced by Frank Tippen of Coventry. These first appeared in 1955, and were one of the earliest full-bodied carriages as well as being an early user of fibreglass construction and the first three-wheel invalid carriage to have sliding doors. The first Deltas had a Villiers Mk 8E engine, wire wheels and a single headlight, and were coloured dark blue. The Delta 2 arrived in 1959 in pale blue with a Villiers Mk 9E, and the Delta 3 gained twin headlights in that same year. A 36-volt electric version was also made from 1965 using the same body for the Ministry of Health. Production of the petrol-powered version ceased in 1970, and the electric one lasted until 1976. The parked car on the right is a 1965 Ford Zephyr.

Above: **Fifteen Weymann Fanfare-bodied Leyland PSUC1/2s, Nos 1130 to 1144 (XUF 130 to 144), were delivered to Southdown between January and March 1960. The original cream window surrounds were repainted light green between 1962 and 1963. This is No 1141 (XUF 141) in the summer of 1967; it remained with Southdown until 1973, when it was withdrawn and sold to Smith of Upper Heyford. It is now in preservation.**

Below: **Between March and July 1961 Southdown took delivery of 30 Harrington Cavalier coach-bodied Leyland L2s, numbered 1700 to 1729 (2700 to 2729 CD); they originally had 28 seats, but many were later re-seated to 41. This is Cheltenham coach station in September 1974, and ready to take up a journey to Brighton is No 1721 (2721 CD).**

Above: **The first full-fronted Northern Counties Leyland PD3/4s arrived in May 1958, and they were first put into service in July 1958 on route 45/45A between Southsea and Warsash. Between October 1960 and May 1961 a batch of 50 Leyland PD3/4s was delivered to Southdown. They were Nos 863 to 912 (2863 to 2912 CD), and passing Eastbourne railway station in May 1972 is No 892 (2892 CD).**

Below: **In March 1961 Southdown received No 894 (2894 CD), and this excellent view of the bus in Terminus Road, Eastbourne, was taken in July 1961. A total of 285 Northern Counties full-front, forward-entrance Leyland PD3/4s were purchased by Southdown between May 1958 and July 1967.**

Above: **Working the high-profile service 31 from Brighton to Southsea in midsummer 1966, with a very healthy passenger load, is No 937 (6937 CD). This bus was part of a large delivery of 40 Northern Counties-bodied Leyland PD3/4s, Nos 913 to 952 (6913 to 6952 CD), that arrived between December 1961 and June 1962. Aldrington Basin, signposted on the extreme left, is the eastern end of the canal that forms part of Shoreham Harbour. An interesting selection of cars on the left includes a Standard 10, a Vauxhall FB, a Ford and the back of a Triumph Herald; to the right are a Ford Corsair and a Mini.**

Below: **Seen at the same location on the same day is No 659 (7659 CD), a Marshall-bodied Leyland PSUC1/1T new to Southdown in April 1962. The overtaking car is an Austin A40 Farina Mark II, which was first available in 1961; the main external differences from the Mark I were a 4-inch increase in wheelbase and a redesigned front grille. The 948cc engine was replaced in the autumn of 1962 by a larger 1,098cc version with an output of 48bhp. The A40 now shared its engine with the recently introduced Morris 1100.**

Above: During April 1962 Southdown took delivery of Nos 655 to 664 (7655 to 7664 CD), which were Marshall-bodied Leyland PSUC1/1Ts. Seen in Horsham in September 1971 is No 660 (7660 CD). Interestingly, to give a comparison of Marshall styles, behind No 660 is a Marshall-bodied Bristol RESL6G, which was part of large batch delivered through the early part of 1968. An excellent mix of cars is also caught by the camera, including a Ford Cortina Mark I on the extreme left, and on the right a two-tone Hillman Minx, an early Vauxhall Viva and, I think, a two-tone Triumph Herald Estate.

Below: Fifteen Weymann coach-bodied Leylands were delivered to Southdown during late 1962. Nos 1145 to 1154 (8145 to 8154 CD) were Leyland PSUC1/2s and Nos 1155 to 1159 (8155 to 8159 CD) were Leyland PSUC3/3R's. About to take up an excursion in the summer of 1967 is No 1154 (8154 CD).

Above: **Twelve Harrington-bodied Leyland Leopard coaches were purchased by Southdown between November 1961 and April 1962. They were numbered 1730 to 1744 (8730 to 8744 CD). The first ten were Leyland L2s with Harrington Cavalier 315 bodywork, and were 31ft 5in long. The last two were Leyland PSU3/3Rs with Harrington Cavalier '36' bodywork with 49 seats. This is No 1743 (8743 CD), one of the 36-foot-long PSU3/3Rs in the summer of 1967. The car to the left is a 1966-registered Hillman Minx Series IV.**

Below: **Arriving at Victoria Coach Station in the summer of 1967 is No 1164 (164 AUF), a Weymann Castillian-bodied Leyland PSU3/3RT new to Southdown in 1963. This bus was part of a batch of 15, Nos 1160 to 1174 (160 to 174 AUF), which was delivered between October 1962 and May 1963. During 1973 No 1164 was sold to Hants & Dorset. The East Kent bus on the right, DJG 630C, is a Park Royal coach-bodied AEC Reliance, new in June 1965.**

Right: **A batch of 20 Marshall BET Leyland PSU3/1Rs with federation-style bodies were delivered to Southdown between May and November 1965. They were numbered 120 to 139 (BUF 120C to 139C), and representing the batch in this view from the summer of 1967 is No 134 (BUF 134C).**

Opposite top: **This is Eastbourne bus station in Cavendish Place in May 1972; I believe it was built in the 1920s. About to depart on service 92 to Hailsham is No 155 (EUF 155D), one of 20 Weymann-bodied Leyland PSU3/1Rs new to Southdown between December 1965 and January 1966. This particular bus was later noted with Stanley Gath of Dewsbury, and subsequently with an Irish operator with a registration of 9584 MI in March 2007. The bus alongside is a Marshall-bodied Leyland PSU3, and to my eye there are two frontal differences, the location of the traffic indicators and the front grille.**

Below: **Thirty-five Northern Counties-bodied Leyland PD3/4s were delivered to Southdown between March and October 1965. They were Nos 250 to 284 (BUF 250C to 284C), and seen in Old Steine, Brighton, in May 1972 is No 255 (BUF 255C).**

Below: **Compare this view of Brighton's Pool Valley taken in May 1973 with the black and white image on page 116. Nearest the camera is No 414 (414 DCD), which was one of a batch of 25 convertible open-top Northern Counties-bodied Leyland PD3/4s new between May and June 1964.**

Above: **Exhibited at the 23rd Earls Court Commercial Motor Show in 1966 was a Northern Counties-bodied Leyland PD3/4 with a full-front wrap-round windscreen and forced ventilation. When delivered to Southdown, the bus was given fleet number 315 and registration number GUF 250D – it was the first Southdown bus since 1944 where none of the digits corresponded with the fleet number. I think this is an excellent view of No 315 in Old Steine in May 1972. The car in the background is, I think, an Aston Martin DB6. From the front, the DB6 looked almost identical to the DB5, the greatest difference being in the rear panels, which incorporated the Kammback, and the DB6 had front-door quarter-lights. The DB6 had a 3,995cc engine producing 282bhp with a top speed of 150mph. Between 1965 and 1971 1,967 DB6s were produced, the last coming of the production line in the first week of January 1971.**

Below: **The last Northern Counties-bodied Leyland PD3/4s delivered to Southdown, with 'panoramic' windows, arrived between February and July 1967. They were Nos 346 to 369 (HCD 346E to 369E), and seen in Shoreham working the long service 31 to Southsea is the brand-new No 366 (HCD 366E). The cars parked on the far side of the road include a Morris Minor, a two-tone 1100 and two Ford Anglias. Following No 366 is an Austin Cambridge and another Morris Minor.**

Above: **In early 1970 Southdown began to take delivery of a batch of coaches with Duple Commander IV bodies on Leyland PSU3A/4R chassis. One of these, No 1813 (RUF 813H) is seen at Tarbet, Scotland, in June 1972.**

Below: **The Tilling group of companies did not wish to purchase Bristol VRT/LLs, with the result that it only received eight completed vehicles by the end of 1968. It used them for training, and no Tilling VRT entered service until after the formation of the National Bus Company in January 1969. Brighton, Hove & District took delivery of ten Bristol VRT/SLs in March and April 1969, but Southdown did not take its first delivery until May and June 1970; these were Nos 501 to 505 (SCD 501H to 505H), Bristol VRTSL2s with Gardner engines. Seen in Old Steine, Brighton, in May 1972 is No 501 (SCD 501H).**

Right: **Another 13 ECW-bodied Bristol VRTSL2s, Nos 506 to 518 (TCD 506J to 509J and UUF 110J to 118J), were delivered to Southdown between September 1970 and April 1971. Seen in Chichester when only five months old is No 514 (UUF 114J). I think the VRT looks so much better in a non-NBC livery.**

Southern Motorways

Below: In 1952, to replace the ageing fleet of Leyland Cubs, London Transport's Country area purchased 84 Guy Special chassis, which were bodied by ECW. They seated 26, were designed for one-person operation, had a Perkins P6 diesel engine, and were put into service between October 1953 and January 1954. In October 1962 there were mass withdrawals of the Guys, with Amersham, Chesham and Epping losing their entire allocation. The last scheduled public service by London Country was on 29 March 1972 on route 336A from Garston. On withdrawal, the type was purchased by a number of smaller operators, mostly around the periphery of London, including Tillingbourne Valley and Southern Motorways. Several Guy Vixens were used by Southern Motorways for services west of Chichester, and this view of GS 2 (MXX 302) was taken in July 1971 in Emsworth Square. New in October 1953, it was initially allocated to Hitchin where it worked on services 383 and 807 until late 1958. By April 1959 it had been transferred to Stevenage, and was there until October 1962. Southern Motorways purchased the bus in June 1963 and it stayed until withdrawal in October 1972, when it passed into private hands for preservation.

Left: In September 1960 Williams of Emsworth purchased a new bus, 650 AAA, a Weymann-bodied Leyland PSUC1/2, and it is seen on a 'private' duty in Portsmouth in July 1971.